God's Message for children

Presented to

_____

by

_____

on the occasion of

_____

dated

_____

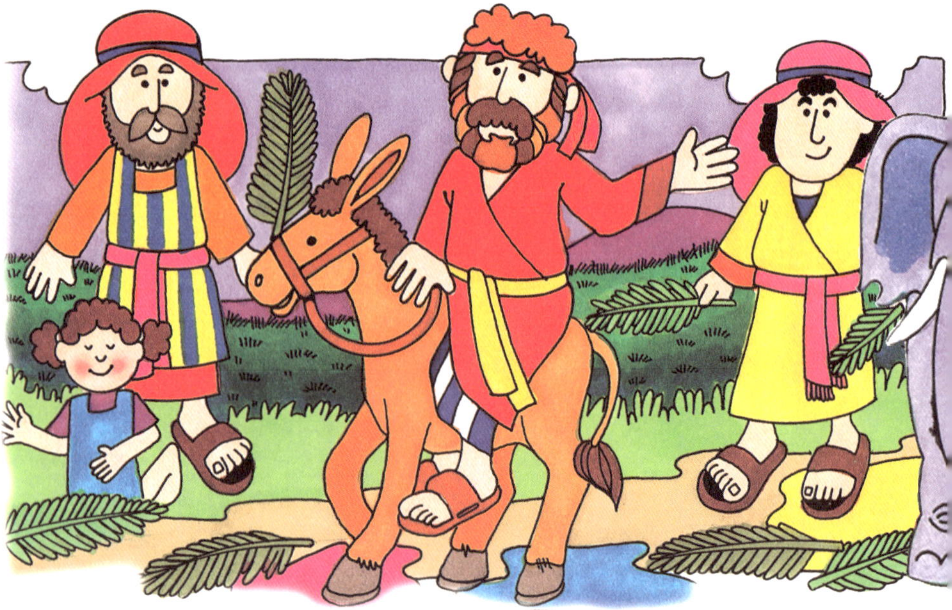

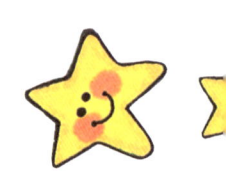

God's Message
for children

CANDLE BOOKS
GRAND RAPIDS, MICHIGAN

Copyright © 1999
CHRISTIAN ART PUBLISHERS
P O Box 1599, Vereeniging, 1930

Illustrations by Theresa Hills

Published in the USA by Candle Books 2001
Distributed by:
Kregel Publications, PO Box 2607
Grand Rapids, Michigan 49501

Scripture quotations taken and adapted from
the Holy Bible, New International Version
Copyright © 1973, 1978, 1984 by
International Bible Society

ISBN 0 8254 7217 2

© All rights reserved. No part of this book may be reproduced in any form without permission in writing from the publisher, except in the case of brief quotations embodied in critical articles or reviews.

Worldwide co-edition arranged by Angus Hudson Ltd,
Concorde House, Mill Hill, London NW7 3SA, England.
Tel: +44 20 8959 3668
Fax: +44 20 8959 3678

Printed in Hong Kong

God's Message for children

God never forsakes his children. He has been there since the beginning. Adam and Eve knew this, Moses saw it when the Red Sea parted before him, Jesus came to show it and Paul told everybody about it. That's why there are so many stories about God's presence and help. In *God's Message for children* every child is invited to join in on the journey through the Bible. With a story for each day of the year God's love and care become evident. Children needn't be afraid, because the Lord is with them.

God's Message for children tries to convey the principles of the Bible in easily understood, everyday English. The passages are short, but long enough to be more than a mere thought, and help children to discover Christ's love in a simple, true-to-Scripture way.

When it all started...

January 1 Genesis 1

In the beginning God created the heavens and the earth. (Gen. 1:1)

God made heaven and the earth a very long time ago. Everything was pitch-dark. There were no people or animals, only water. Then God said, "Let there be light!" and suddenly everything was bright. God was happy with the light.

The next day God decided to make the sky that we see above us every day. On the third day God gathered all the water together into one place and called it the "sea". The dry ground He named "land". On that same day God also made all the plants and trees.

At the start of the fourth day, God decided to make the sun so it could shine during the day. He also made the moon and the stars to shine at night.

On the fifth day God made all the sea creatures and fish and every kind of bird.

On the sixth day God said, "Let there be animals on earth." The next moment there were animals as far as the eye could see. The whole earth was now full of life. It was very beautiful.

Remember: Our God is a powerful God. He created everything.

The Lord makes people

January 2 Genesis 1

"Let's make people to take care of the earth for Us." (Gen. 1:26)

It took God six days to make the world. There were all sorts of plants, fish and animals but no people so, on the sixth day, God decided to make people. The first man and woman God made were His most important creation. God was so proud of Adam and Eve that He put them in charge of everything on earth. They were God's representatives and the world was in their hands.

God told Adam and Eve to look after the world and to have children so that, in time, there would be people all over the world. God made sure there was enough food for them to eat. They ate the grain and fruit that grew on the plants and trees. The animals and birds ate grass and leafy plants.

Everything started off well. The first people were more important to God than anything else He had created. God wanted them to take good care of the earth and we need to do the same. Every single part of the world belongs to God, including all the animals and plants. That's why we should not spoil His world by being greedy and wasteful. We should work with nature and protect what God has given us.

Remember: People are God's most important creation.

God rests

January 3 Genesis 2

On the seventh day God had finished with everything He made. Then He rested after all the hard work. (Gen. 2:2)

In six days God made all that we see around us as well as everything we don't see. God is so mighty and powerful that He holds the whole world in His hand. His Name is written on the whole universe.

When God finished making everything, He decided to rest and He told the people to rest from their work every seventh day. This was to be a special day.

Today we Christians have our day of rest on Sundays because this is the day when Jesus rose from the dead. It's a day when we can be together with our families and when we can go to church and give thanks for all the wonderful things that the Lord has made. And, on Sundays and every other day, we should help others and pray for people who are suffering or in trouble.

Remember: We serve God seven days a week.

The Lord gives Adam a wife

January 4 Genesis 2

"At last!" Adam exclaimed. "The Lord has made someone just like me. She will be called 'woman.'" (Gen. 2:23)

The story of how God made the world is so awesome that it is told twice, in the first two chapters of Genesis. In Genesis 2 we read about the beautiful Garden of Eden, and how God told Adam, the first human being, that he could live there and take care of the garden.

One day God decided that it was not good for Adam to be all alone. So He made animals and birds and Adam had to choose names for them. But Adam was still the only human being.

So the Lord put Adam to sleep. Then He took one of Adam's ribs and made a woman from it. The Lord brought the woman to Adam. Adam was pleased to have someone like him on earth. From now on the woman would help him and he wouldn't be on his own any more.

The very first wedding took place in Eden. Before there was any sin or death in the world, God brought the first man and woman together. Adam said something very important about marriage. He said grown-ups who get married should love each other forever and stay together for the rest of their lives.

Remember: We should love other people and help them.

Adam and Eve make the Lord very sad

January 5 Genesis 3

"It's only the fruit from the tree in the middle of the garden that we are not allowed to eat. God says we should not eat it or even touch it, or we will die." (Gen. 3:3)

The snake wanted to get Eve into trouble. He asked her, "Did God really say you shouldn't eat any of the fruit in the garden?" She told him they could eat all the fruit except the fruit from the tree in the middle of the garden. "You won't die if you eat it!" the snake hissed. He told Eve that she and Adam should eat the fruit because then they would become like God.

Without thinking twice, Adam and Eve started eating the fruit God told them not to eat. Instantly their eyes were opened. They saw for the first time that they had no clothes on. That evening Adam and Eve tried to hide away from God in the garden when He came looking for them. God asked them what they had done. Adam said it was all Eve's fault. Eve blamed the snake.

The Lord was very sad. He put a curse on the snake. He told Eve that she would suffer a lot of pain when she had babies. Adam's punishment was that he would have to work very hard to make a living. The first people on earth really made a mess of things and to this day we have to pay for what they did. Fortunately God still cares for us.

Remember: God's children should obey God.

A second chance

January 6 Genesis 3-4

The Lord told Adam and his wife to get out of the Garden of Eden. They had to work the land outside Eden from now on. (Gen. 3:23)

The first human beings had the chance of a lifetime and they let it slip through their fingers. They had to live outside Eden because they had disobeyed God but God gave them another chance. He did not destroy the world and Adam and Eve were still alive, even if they weren't allowed in Eden.

Unfortunately, they still hadn't learned their lesson. One day Cain and Abel, Adam and Eve's sons, each brought the Lord an offering. The Lord accepted Abel's offering, but not Cain's. This made Cain so angry that he attacked and killed his brother. They were barely out of Eden, and already someone had been murdered!

We all do wrong things that hurt the Lord, but our God is a good God. He doesn't give up on us when we do something wrong. He gives us another chance. He even sent His son, Jesus, to die on the cross for us. We can take all our sins to Him and ask for forgiveness. In the Bible it says Jesus promises to forgive us if we are really sorry for what we have done.

Remember: God loves all His children.

Noah builds an ark

January 7 Genesis 6-7

Noah was a man who did what God said. There was no one like him on earth at the time. He was very close to God. (Gen. 6:9)

The world had become a rotten and violent place because of the people's sins and it broke God's heart. He almost wished He hadn't made people. God decided He was going to get rid of all the people on earth. But there was one man who obeyed God—Noah. So God decided to let Noah and his family live. As for the rest of the world—a flood would destroy every creature on earth.

The Lord told Noah to build a big boat from wood. We call it an ark. Noah had to take a pair of every kind of animal—a male and a female—into the ark with him. This was to make sure that there would be animals and birds on earth again after the flood. God reminded Noah to take enough food for his family and the animals.

It rained for forty days and forty nights. The waters rose higher and higher until they covered even the highest mountains. The flood lasted another one hundred and fifty days. Every living thing died. Only Noah, and those he took with him in the ark, were left alive. God took good care of them.

Remember: We are supposed to obey God every day.

The waters start going down

January 8 Genesis 8

The Lord was pleased with Noah's offering. He said to Himself, "I will never again send something as bad as this flood. Not even if people do wicked things." (Gen. 8:21)

Slowly but surely the water was receding. One day Noah opened the window in the ark and released a raven. Then he sent a dove out to see if it could find dry ground. It couldn't, so it flew back to the ark. Seven days later Noah sent the dove out again. Towards evening, the dove came back with an olive leaf in its beak and Noah knew that the water was almost gone. A week later he sent out the dove once more. This time it didn't return, so Noah opened up the ark.

Noah was happy that the Lord had let them live. He brought the Lord an offering to thank Him. This pleased the Lord and He promised that the world would never see such a disaster again.

God is such a good God. He loves each one of us so much and He is happy when we listen to Him every day.

Remember: We have to look after what God has made.

God's rainbow is meant for all of us

January 9 Genesis 9

"I will not break the agreement I make with you. I promise never to send another flood to kill all people and animals and destroy the earth. Never again will there be so much water in one place on earth." (Gen. 9:11)

God blessed Noah and his family to show how much He loved them. He gave them plants, animals, birds and fish for food. But He warned them never to kill another human being.

Then God made an agreement with Noah and his sons. It was called a covenant. God promised never to send a flood to destroy the whole world again. God gave them a sign to prove that He would keep His promise. The sign was a rainbow. When we see a rainbow in the sky after it rains, we remember that God is still keeping His promise to Noah. Since the flood in Noah's time there has never been so much water at one time in any place on earth. After it rains, look for a rainbow. It reminds us of how much God still cares for us all.

God doesn't spy on us or try to catch us doing bad things. He wants us to be close to Him. We must put our hand in His every day because He loves us.

Remember: God always does what He says He will do.

People aren't as great as they think they are

January 10 Genesis 11

"Come, let's go down and give them different languages. Then they won't be able to understand each other." (Gen. 11:7)

A long time ago, people all over the world spoke the same language, so they all understood one another. One day, to show how smart and important they were, they decided to build a huge city with a tower that would reach to the sky. The Lord came down to see the city and the tower that was being built and He was not impressed. He didn't like the way the people were showing off so He decided to mix up their words. Suddenly everyone started speaking different languages. They couldn't understand each other and that ended their building project. The city where they built the tower was called Babel.

People moved away from Babel to different places around the world. There was no reason to stay together if they couldn't understand each other. This was God's way of punishing them for thinking that they were so important.

Remember: God wants us to be humble.

God's new hero: Abram

January 11 Genesis 12-13

"Leave your country, your people and your family. Go to the land I will show you." (Gen. 12:1)

One day the Lord went to the land of Ur to tell Abram that He wanted him to move away. Abram obeyed God right away. When he finally arrived in Canaan, God told him that this land would belong to his family some day. He also said, "I will bless you and make you famous." Abram built an altar to thank and worship the Lord.

Later on Abram and his wife Sarai went down to Egypt. Sarai was very beautiful and the Egyptian king married her. He thought she was Abram's sister, but the Lord punished the king for what he did. The king was angry and asked Abram why he hadn't told him Sarai was his wife. Then he told them to leave Egypt right away.

Yet again God told Abram that he would have very many grandchildren and the family line would go on and on. Wherever Abram went, the Lord was with him.

We who believe in the Lord are also part of Abram's family and proof of how God kept His promise to Abram. God is our Father who cares for us.

Remember: We have a Father in heaven who loves us.

January 12 Genesis 15

Abram will have a big family

The Lord brought Abram outside beneath the night sky and told him, "Look up into the heavens and count the stars if you can. Your descendants will be like that—too many to count!" (Gen. 15:5)

One day the Lord spoke to Abram again. He told him again that he would be the father of a great nation. But Abram and his wife were childless and he reminded God of this fact. Still the Lord made him look up at the sky and promised Abram that he would have more descendants than he could count—as many as the stars. Abram believed Him and this made the Lord happy.

That day the Lord made another covenant with Abram to prove that He would keep His promise. Abram had to kill a ram, a goat and a heifer and cut each one open, in two halves. Then, as the sun was going down, Abram fell asleep.

After the sun had set, Abram saw a smoking fire-pot and a flaming torch pass between the pieces of meat. This was the sign that someday God would give Abram his own country and many descendants.

God never lies. Sometimes it takes a while for His promises to happen, but we have to be patient. We should not doubt God even when times are hard. He sees everything and cares for us. As long as we hold on to His hand, He won't let us down.

Remember: God will never stop loving us.

The Lord speaks to Abram again

January 13 Genesis 17

Then God said to Abram, "This is my covenant with you: you will be the father of many nations." (Gen. 17:4)

When Abram was ninety-nine years old, the Lord spoke to him. He told Abram, once again, that he would have many descendants. But by this time Abram had given up hope. He and his wife were already very old. As Abram bowed down, he laughed softly to himself. How on earth would it be possible for him and Sarai to have a child at this age? So Abram asked the Lord to bless Ishmael, the son he had by the slave Hagar.

But the Lord had His own plans. He replied that soon Sarai would have a son and that they were to name him Isaac. The name means "he laughs". That would always remind Abram that he doubted God's word.

God then changed Abram's name to Abraham, because he would be the father of many nations. Sarai's name was changed to Sarah, because she would soon give birth to Isaac. The Lord also told Abraham that from now on every baby boy had to be circumcised on the eighth day after his birth, including the baby boys of slaves who lived in their homes. This would be the sign of God's covenant with Abraham.

Remember: We should believe what God tells us.

Abraham prays for Sodom

January 14 Genesis 18-19

Finally Abraham said, "Lord, please do not get angry! May I speak one more time? Suppose there are ten good people in Sodom?" The Lord answered, "If there are ten good people I will not destroy the city." (Gen. 18:32)

One day the Lord told Abraham He had heard that the people of Sodom and Gomorrah were evil, so He had decided to destroy the two cities.

Abraham's nephew Lot and his family lived there, so he pleaded with the Lord, "Suppose You find 50 good people in the city—will You still destroy it?" The Lord promised to spare the whole city if He found 50 good people in Sodom.

Abraham went on, "Suppose there are only 45?" The Lord said He would spare Sodom for the sake of 45 good people. But Abraham still didn't give up. Would the Lord spare Sodom if there were only ten good people in it? Again the Lord's answer was "yes."

Eventually the Lord did destroy Sodom and Gomorrah in a huge fire. But first He sent His angels to tell Lot and his family to run for their lives. The angel also warned them not to look back at the city while it was burning. Lot's wife didn't obey, so she was punished. She was turned into a pillar of salt.

Remember: God must come first in our lives.

Abraham is willing to sacrifice Isaac

January 15 Genesis 22

Then God said, "Put down the knife. Don't kill your son, because now I know that you truly serve Me. You were even willing to sacrifice your only son for Me." (Gen. 22:12)

One day God told Abraham to go and sacrifice Isaac on a mountain in the land of Moriah. Abraham and Isaac left early the next morning. It took them three days to reach the mountain.

While they were on their way, Isaac asked his father, "We have the wood and the fire, but where is the lamb for the sacrifice?" Abraham told him not to worry, because the Lord would take care of it.

When they arrived at the place for the sacrifice, Abraham tied Isaac up and laid him on the altar on top of the wood. Abraham took his knife and was about to kill his son when an angel of the Lord spoke to him from heaven. The angel told him to put down the knife and not to kill the boy. Then the Lord sent a ram to sacrifice instead of Isaac.

Abraham proved that he was willing to do anything the Lord asked—even sacrifice his son. We must also give our whole lives to the Lord. We must love God best of all because He loves us so much.

Remember: God must be the most important Person in our lives.

Isaac finds a wife

January 16 Genesis 24

"O Lord, God of my master Abraham, please give me a miracle today." (Gen. 24:12)

When Abraham was a very old man, he called his servant and told him to go to Mesopotamia to find Isaac a wife.

The servant went to the village Nahor, where some of Abraham's relations lived. Standing beside a spring where the young girls of the village came to get water, he prayed for a miracle. He asked the Lord to show him a girl who would be the right wife for Isaac. He would ask for a drink and the girl who said, "Yes, certainly, and I will water your camels too," would be the one. As he was still praying, he saw a girl named Rebekah arrive with a water jug on her shoulder. He went over to her and asked for a drink of water.

She gave the right answer, so the servant knew she was the girl. He gave her some expensive jewelry and she took him to her brother Laban's house. When the servant told Laban and his mother how the Lord had guided him in a special way, they were very happy.

They allowed Rebekah to go back with him.

Rebekah went to live with Sarah. Later on she and Isaac got married. Isaac loved Rebekah very much.

Remember: The Lord looks after His children.

Jacob is blessed instead of Esau

January 17 Genesis 27

God gives you plenty of dew for healthy crops and good harvests; you will always have enough to eat. (Gen. 27:28)

After Abraham's death, his son Isaac and Rebekah had twins. They called them Esau and Jacob. By the time they were grown up, Isaac was almost blind. One day Isaac told Esau to hunt some wild game for him. He asked his son to cook it the way he liked it. Afterwards, he would bless Esau.

Rebekah heard what Isaac said. She wanted their younger son, Jacob, to be blessed. So she made a plan. She sent Jacob to get a goat so she could cook Isaac's favorite dish. Jacob would take the food to his father and pretend to be Esau. Then Isaac would bless him instead.

Rebekah told Jacob to wear Esau's clothes, and she draped the goat's skin on his arms and neck because Esau was very hairy. Her plan worked! Esau's father couldn't bless him now, because the blessing was meant for only one son.

Esau was furious with Jacob. He wanted to kill him. Rebekah told Jacob to run away, so Jacob went to live with his uncle, Laban. In the end, the Lord's promise to Abraham came true.

Remember: We should always be honest.

Jacob's dream

January 18 Genesis 28

At the top of the stairway stood the Lord, and He said, "I am the Lord, the God of your grandfather Abraham and the God of your father, Isaac. The ground you are lying on belongs to you. I will give it to you and your descendants." (Gen. 28:13)

Jacob was on his way to his uncle Laban's house. At sunset he arrived at a good place to set up camp and spend the night. As he slept, he dreamed of a stairway that reached from the earth to heaven. The angels of God were going up and down the stairs. The Lord stood at the top of the stairway and spoke to Jacob. God promised to be his God as well. Everything He had promised his grandparents would also come true for Jacob. Jacob's descendants would get the land the Lord had promised them.

The Lord also promised Jacob in his dream that he would never be alone again. God would be with him all the time.

When Jacob woke up, he was afraid. He said, "What an awesome place this is!" He couldn't believe that the Lord was there and he didn't even know it! Early the next morning Jacob named the place Bethel. This means "house of God". There Jacob made a vow that he would serve God.

The Lord is with us every day of our lives. We are never alone. He sees everything we do, and He hears everything we say.

Remember: The Lord knows everything about us.

The dreamer is sold

January 19 Genesis 37

Joseph had a dream and told his brothers, "Listen to this dream. We were out in the field tying up bundles of grain. My bundle stood up, and then your bundles all gathered around and bowed low before it!" (Gen. 37:6-7)

Jacob had many sons but he loved Joseph more than the others. This made Joseph's brothers jealous of him. One night Joseph dreamed that his brothers' sheaves of corn bowed down to his sheaf of corn. In another dream, the sun, moon and eleven stars bowed low before him. He described these dreams to his brothers in detail, and then they liked him even less.

Soon after this, Joseph's brothers were taking care of the flocks. Jacob sent Joseph to see how they were doing. When his brothers saw Joseph coming, they decided to kill him. But thanks to Reuben, they threw him into a pit instead. A while later, some traders came by. Joseph's brothers dragged him out of the pit and sold him to the traders.

Then Joseph's brothers dipped his clothes in a goat's blood and told their father that a wild animal must have eaten him. Meanwhile, the traders sold Joseph to Potiphar. Potiphar was captain of the Egyptian king's palace guard.

Remember: The Lord loves everybody in our family.

Joseph ends up in prison

January 20 Genesis 39-40

While Joseph was in prison, the Lord was with him all the time. The Lord was good to Joseph. After a while even the chief jailer liked him. (Gen. 39:20-21)

In Egypt, Joseph worked in Potiphar's house. Potiphar's wife really liked him. She even wanted him to be her boyfriend, but Joseph refused. Eventually she became so angry that she told her husband lies about Joseph. Potiphar believed his wife. He threw Joseph into prison.

The lesson we learn from Joseph is never to listen to friends or anybody who tries to talk us into doing something wrong—even if it means being punished for something we didn't do. We must listen only to the Lord.

God was with Joseph in prison. Some time later, Pharaoh's cupbearer and chief baker were put in the same prison as Joseph. One morning the two of them told Joseph about the weird dreams that they had the night before. Joseph explained the meaning of their dreams to them. He told the cupbearer he would be back in the palace within three days, pouring Pharaoh's wine again. But the baker's news was not so good. He would be dead within three days! Everything happened exactly as Joseph had said.

Remember: The Lord is pleased with those who obey Him.

Joseph explains Pharaoh's dreams

January 21 Genesis 41

"I had a dream last night," Pharaoh told Joseph, "and nobody can tell me what it means. I hear that you can explain dreams." Joseph said to Pharaoh, "I can't do it. God gives me the answers." (Gen. 41:15-16)

One night Pharaoh had a dream. In his dream, seven fat, healthy-looking cows came up from the river and started grazing. Then seven ugly, skinny cows came along and ate the fat ones. Later that night he dreamed about seven full heads of grain on one stalk. Then seven shriveled-up heads of grain swallowed up the healthy ones.

Pharaoh wondered what these dreams could mean. The man who poured Pharaoh's wine in the palace remembered Joseph in prison. Pharaoh sent for Joseph at once. The dreams meant that there would be seven good years in Egypt with plenty of rain and more than enough food followed by seven years of famine. Pharaoh was so pleased with Joseph that he gave him a very important job. Only Pharaoh had a higher rank than Joseph.

Joseph's story tells us that the Lord uses people anywhere, even in prison. We need to believe in Him no matter where we are.

Remember: The Lord is with us wherever we go.

Joseph's brothers come to buy food in Egypt

January 22 Genesis 42-43

Joseph put his brothers in prison for three days. On the third day Joseph said to them, "I serve God. If you do as I say, you will live. One of you must stay behind in prison. The rest of you may go on home with grain for your families." (Gen. 42:17, 19)

When the seven years of famine and suffering began, Joseph started selling grain. One day Joseph's brothers arrived from Canaan to buy food. Joseph recognized them immediately, but they didn't recognize him at all. Joseph pretended that he thought they had come to spy on the land and start a war with Egypt, and he put them in prison.

Three days later, Joseph allowed all but one of his brothers to go home. They had to get their younger brother, Benjamin, and bring him to Joseph. Then they wouldn't be hurt.

Meanwhile, Joseph secretly put the money his brothers had paid for the grain into their sacks of grain. His brothers were terrified when they discovered the money. Back home in Canaan, they told their father what had happened. At first Jacob refused to send Benjamin to Egypt, but his sons pleaded with him and eventually he let them take Benjamin.

Joseph was very happy to see Benjamin. He invited his brothers to a grand meal in the palace, but he still didn't tell them who he really was.

Remember: The Lord cares about even the smallest child.

Joseph helps his brothers

January 23 Genesis 44-45

"I am Joseph!" he said to his brothers. (Gen. 45:3)

Joseph's brothers were ready to leave for Canaan with the grain. This time Joseph secretly had his own silver cup hidden in Benjamin's sack. The brothers were barely out of the city when Joseph's household manager caught up with them and stopped them: "What do you mean by stealing my master's silver drinking cup?" the man said. Whoever had stolen it would have to stay behind in Egypt as a slave.

The cup was found in Benjamin's sack. The brothers were devastated. Judah told Joseph how heartbroken their father would be if they returned without Benjamin.

Eventually Joseph could stand it no longer. He decided to tell them who he was. His brothers were amazed and afraid. Joseph told them not to worry. He wasn't angry with them anymore. His going to Egypt had been part of God's plan. He told them to hurry home and get their father so they could live together in Egypt.

God has a plan for each of us. If we listen to Him, He will do great things in our lives.

Remember: God never stops changing people.

Joseph meets Jacob

January 24 Genesis 46-47

Then Jacob said to Joseph, "Now I can die, because I have seen you with my own eyes and know you are still alive." (Gen. 46:30)

Back home in Canaan, Joseph's brothers told their father what had happened. Jacob couldn't wait to see Joseph again.

Jacob and his whole family left for Egypt. Joseph was so happy when he saw his father that he gave him a big hug and cried with joy. Later on Joseph brought his father to Pharaoh so they could meet each other.

Pharaoh gave them the land called Goshen and they lived there happily for many years. When Jacob was very old and it was time for him to die, he called for all his sons and blessed them. After Jacob's death Joseph buried him in Canaan. Then he went back to Egypt.

Joseph's life wasn't always easy, but it shows us how great the Lord is. He used Joseph in a truly wonderful way. God showed His great power through the life of one man who loved Him!

Remember: God cares for the young and the old.

Another hero is born

January 25 Exodus 2

The princess named him Moses, because "I took him out of the water." (Exod. 2:10)

After Joseph's death there was a new king in Egypt. He knew nothing about Joseph and he didn't like the Israelites one bit. There were too many of them for his liking, so Pharaoh decided they had to work as slaves. On top of that, all baby boys born to the Israelites had to be thrown into the River Nile.

During this time an Israelite mother made a plan to save her baby son's life. She made a basket of reeds and waterproofed it with tar and pitch. Then she put her baby in the basket, among the reeds on the riverbank.

Soon afterwards, one of Pharaoh's daughters went to swim in the river. She saw the basket with the baby inside and decided to keep him. Just then the baby's sister ran up to the princess and said, "I can get someone to take care of the baby until he is older." The princess was pleased. So the baby was taken to his own mother, who looked after him until he was old enough to live in the palace.

Pharaoh's daughter decided to call the baby Moses.

Remember: God can save us from the greatest danger.

Moses kills an Egyptian and makes a getaway

January 26 Exodus 2

The man said to Moses, "Do you plan to kill me as you killed that Egyptian yesterday?" (Exod. 2:14)

Moses was raised in Pharaoh's palace. One day, when he was already grown up, he walked among the Israelites and saw how hard they were forced to work. The next moment he saw an Egyptian beating an Israelite. Moses was so angry that he killed the Egyptian. He quickly buried him in the sand.

The next day Moses paid another visit to his people. This time he saw two Israelites fighting. He told them to stop. "Who do you think you are?" one of the men asked Moses. "Do you plan to kill me as you killed that Egyptian yesterday?"

When Moses realized that people knew what he had done, he was worried. His life was in danger. And sure enough, when Pharaoh heard about it, he gave orders for Moses to be killed. So Moses fled to the land of Midian.

One day Moses helped some girls get water from a well for their flocks. When they told their father about this, he invited Moses to come and stay with them. Later on, Moses married one of the man's daughters, Zipporah.

We can't get away with doing wrong. Even if nobody sees us, God sees everything. We can't hide anything from Him.

Remember: We shouldn't fight with our friends.

God calls Moses

January 27 Exodus 3

"Do not come any closer," God told him. "Take off your sandals because you are standing on holy ground." (Exod. 3:5)

Moses looked after the flock of his father-in-law, Jethro. One day a strange thing happened. At Mount Horeb he saw a burning bush. But it did not burn up. Moses went closer to see what was going on. Suddenly a voice called to him from the bush, "Moses! Moses!"

He answered right away, "Here I am."

Then God told him not to come any closer—he was on holy ground.

God told Moses how sorry He felt for the people of Israel. He had decided to send Moses to go and set them free. This scared Moses. "I can't do this," Moses said. "I'm not important enough."

God said, "I will be with you."

Moses asked God His name. "I am who I am," was the Lord's answer.

That day, at the burning bush, Moses heard that God's name is "Lord". This name is so important that we have to be careful how we use it. His name is holy. Only people who believe in Him and really love Him are allowed to call God by His name.

Remember: God's name is a holy name.

The Lord shows Moses that He will help him

January 28 Exodus 4

The Lord said to Moses, "Go now, and do as I have told you. I will help you speak well, and I will tell you what to say." (Exod. 4:12)

Moses was frightened when the Lord spoke to him from the burning bush. He asked the Lord, "If I go to the people of Israel and tell them You sent me, they won't believe me. Then what should I tell them?"

So God gave Moses three signs to show that He was with him. These were the signs: when Moses threw his shepherd's staff onto the ground, it changed into a snake; when Moses put his hand inside his clothes and took it out again, it was white with leprosy; when Moses poured water from the Nile onto the ground, it changed into blood.

But Moses was still worried. "Oh, Lord, I'm just not a good speaker. I'm clumsy with words." The Lord answered, "I will help you speak well, and I will tell you what to say." The Lord also told Moses to go get his brother, Aaron. Aaron would go to Egypt with Moses and speak for him.

Moses and Aaron set off on their journey to the Israelites. When Moses performed the miracles God had given him, they believed him. They accepted him as their leader.

Remember: We can help God just as we are.

Moses speaks to Pharaoh

January 29 Exodus 5-6

"Now you will see what I will do to Pharaoh," the Lord told Moses. *"I will force him to let the people go."* (Exod. 6:1)

Moses and Aaron went to see the king of Egypt. They told him that the Lord wanted the people of Israel to leave Egypt. They had to hold a religious festival in the desert in God's honor.

Pharaoh's answer was, "And who is the Lord that I should listen to Him and let Israel go? I don't know the Lord, and I will not let Israel go."

Moses tried again, but Pharaoh was stubborn. He decided to make the Israelites work even harder. So Pharaoh told his foremen, "Don't give the people straw for making bricks anymore. Let them get it themselves!" And they had to make just as many bricks as before.

The poor Israelites had to work harder than ever. They got angry with Moses and Aaron. They blamed Moses. They wouldn't even listen when Moses told them that the Lord would help them.

Sometimes, when bad things happen to us, it isn't easy to believe in the Lord. At times like that we shouldn't think that God has forgotten about us. He is with His children all the time.

Remember: We should never stop believing in the Lord.

Moses and Pharaoh's magicians

January 30 Exodus 7

When I show the Egyptians my power and force them to let the Israelites go, they will realize that I am the Lord. (Exod. 7:5)

Once again the Lord sent Moses and Aaron to Pharaoh. Because Moses did not speak well, Aaron spoke for him. Moses was eighty and Aaron was eighty-three. The Lord told them beforehand that Pharaoh would not listen to them. He was too stubborn. That's why the Lord would punish him. Later on Pharaoh would give in and allow the Israelites to leave.

Moses and Aaron went to Pharaoh's palace. Aaron threw Moses' staff on the ground before Pharaoh and it changed into a snake. Pharaoh's magicians did the same thing. Their staffs became snakes too! But then Aaron's snake swallowed up their snakes.

Pharaoh wouldn't listen to Moses. Not even after seeing this sign. So Moses and Aaron left.

Just like Pharaoh, there are many people today who don't believe in God. Even if they see miracles, they couldn't care less. We need to pray for them and ask the Lord to change their lives so that they will also believe in Him. Otherwise they are going to be punished someday. God doesn't want people to be punished, but to belong to Him forever.

Remember: God wants all people to become His children.

The Lord sends plagues to punish Pharaoh

January 31 Exodus 7-9

Suddenly gnats were all over the place, covering the Egyptians and their animals. "This is the finger of God!" Pharaoh's magicians told him. (Exod. 8:17)

Pharaoh didn't want to listen to Moses and Aaron, so the Lord sent ten plagues over Egypt. The first plague struck the River Nile. The water turned to blood. Nobody could drink it, but Pharaoh still wouldn't listen.

Then the Lord sent a plague of frogs. Pharaoh asked Moses to pray that the frogs would go away and then he would let the people go. But he lied!

Then the Lord sent a plague of gnats. Everybody was covered with gnats! But Pharaoh was still stubborn.

Next came a plague of flies. Eventually Pharaoh said it was all right for the Israelites to offer sacrifices to God, but they had to do it in Egypt. But Moses replied, "That won't do! We must take a three-day trip into the wilderness." Pharaoh agreed, but he didn't mean it.

The Lord sent yet another plague, which affected the livestock. All the Egyptians' animals died. But Pharaoh still had a heart of stone.

Remember: People who do bad things make God unhappy.

More plagues

February 1 Exodus 9-10

God said to Pharaoh, "There is only one reason why I have let you live. Through you I will show my strength. Then the entire world will see how great I am." (Exod. 9:16)

The first five plagues were not enough to make Pharaoh listen, so God sent five more. The sixth was a plague of boils that broke out on all the people and animals in Egypt. But once again, Pharaoh's heart was hard.

Then a seventh plague struck—a tremendous hailstorm. Pharaoh urgently sent for Moses and said the Israelites could go at once. But he was lying again!

Moses asked Pharaoh how long he was going to continue refusing to listen to the Lord. So Pharaoh said the men could go, but the women and children had to stay behind. Moses wasn't happy with this, but Pharaoh just shouted, "Get out of here!"

Moses raised his staff over the land of Egypt. Then a plague of locusts swarmed over the land. There were so many of them, you couldn't see the ground. This was the eighth plague. Once again Pharaoh asked Moses to pray that the locusts go away.

The ninth plague was three days of darkness. The people scarcely moved because they couldn't see. After this plague Pharaoh said the Israelites could go. But their flocks and herds had to stay. Moses refused.

Remember: Pray for sinners to believe in the Lord.

The tenth plague

February 2 Exodus 11-12

And at midnight the Lord killed all the eldest sons in Egypt, from Pharaoh's son to those in prison. Even the eldest of their livestock were killed. (Exod. 12:29)

Not even the ninth plague softened Pharaoh's heart. He shouted at Moses, "Don't ever let me see you again! The day I do, you will die!" Then the Lord told Moses He would send one more plague—at midnight all the eldest children in every family would die. The Egyptians would be heartbroken and their crying and wailing would be heard throughout the land. Not a single Israelite child would die. Then Pharaoh would allow the Israelites to leave Egypt. Moses went and told Pharaoh all this but Pharaoh still wouldn't listen, and Moses walked out, burning with anger.

At midnight, the tenth plague struck Egypt. Every eldest son in every family, from the richest to the poorest, died. Even the oldest male animals died.

The Lord showed the Egyptians His power with all the plagues He sent. He did this to save the people He loved so much.

God still watches over us today. He cares for us. He takes us by the hand. God will never punish us the way He did the bad Egyptian king.

Remember: The Lord cares a lot about His children.

The first Passover

February 3 Exodus 12

"The blood you have smeared above your doors will be a sign. When I see the blood I will pass over you. This plague of death will not touch you when I strike the land of Egypt." (Exod. 12:13)

The day before the Lord struck Egypt with the tenth plague, He told the Israelites to celebrate this day as a special festival. Every family had to slaughter a lamb. That evening everyone would eat roast lamb with herbs and bread made without yeast. This was the feast of the Passover.

That night in Egypt, the Israelites had to take some of the lambs' blood and smear it above the doors of their houses. This was the sign to show the Lord that Israelites lived there. No one in that house would die.

The Israelites celebrated the Passover feast in Egypt, and the Lord told them to celebrate it every year from that time on. This festival would remind them of the night the Lord freed them from the Egyptians. They also had to explain the meaning of the ceremony to their children. Then they would always remember how the Lord saved their lives the night God sent the tenth plague to Egypt.

The Israelites were very happy. They bowed their heads and worshipped the Lord. Then they celebrated the Passover feast.

Remember: Religious feasts remind us about God's salvation.

The Israelites move out of Egypt

February 4 Exodus 13

So God led them along a route through the wilderness towards the Red Sea, and the Israelites left Egypt like a marching army. (Exod. 13:18)

The tenth plague was just too much for Pharaoh. He couldn't stand it any longer. So he sent for Moses and Aaron during the night. "Leave us!" he cried. "Go away, all of you! Go and serve the Lord. Take your flocks and herds and get out of here."

The Egyptians even gave the Israelites expensive clothes and jewelry to take with them! There were almost six hundred thousand men, not counting the women and children. They took all their animals with them. After 430 years the Israelites were finally moving out of Egypt!

God led the Israelites along a route through the wilderness towards the Red Sea. It wasn't the shortest way, but it was the safest. Because it was so hot, the Lord sent a big cloud to give them shade during the day. At night God sent a huge ball of fire so they could see where they were going. God keeps His promises. Even if we sometimes get impatient, we just need to keep on trusting Him.

Remember: Even if it takes a long time, God always keeps His promises.

Pharaoh drowns in the sea

February 5 Exodus 14

Then Moses raised his hand over the sea, and the Lord opened up a path through the water with a strong east wind. (Exod. 14:21)

When Pharaoh realized the Israelites weren't coming back, he was sorry he had let them go. "What have we done, letting all these slaves get away?" So Pharaoh called out his troops and a mighty Egyptian army chased after the Israelites. But the Lord watched over His people. An angel moved in behind the Israelites, and so did the cloud. Everything in front of the Egyptians was dark.

Moses and the Israelites arrived at the Red Sea. Then Moses raised his hand over the sea and a miracle happened. The sea opened up before them so they could walk through on dry ground with water on each side! The Egyptians followed them, but their chariot wheels got stuck. Then the Lord told Moses to raise his hand over the sea again. The water flooded back and all the Egyptians drowned. It was another miracle.

The Lord can do anything. He can even dry up the sea if He wants to. If we look around us we will see plenty of miracles. We can trust the Lord to perform miracles in our lives too!

Remember: The Lord still does great things today.

The Israelites thank the Lord

February 6 Exodus 15

Then Moses said, "I want to sing a song to the Lord. He is mighty! He can throw horses and chariots into the sea." (Exod. 15:1)

The Israelites walked through the sea without even getting wet, but all the Egyptians died. The Israelites could hardly believe that the Lord had been so good to them. They actually saw Him perform a miracle before their very eyes. He saved them from the mighty Egyptian army and they hadn't even had to fight. The Lord did this for them!

On the other side of the Red Sea, Moses and the people sang a song to thank the Lord for saving them. In the song they sang about God's greatness and His power. His hand smashes the enemy to pieces. With just one word from God, the wind blows them over and the sea swallows them up.

There is nobody like the Lord. He is the strongest, the best! He is our God too. He cares for us. God is the most important Person there is. He is our heavenly Father. He is never too busy to listen to us. All we have to do is kneel down before Him. Then He hears every word we say to Him.

Remember: We should ask the Lord every day to take care of our families.

Bitter water made sweet

February 7 Exodus 15

Moses prayed to the Lord and the Lord showed him a branch. Moses took the branch and threw it into the water. This made the water taste good. (Exod. 15:25)

The Israelites traveled in the desert for three days without water. When they came to a place called Marah, they finally found water. But they couldn't drink it because it had a bitter taste. So they complained. "What are we going to drink?" they asked Moses.

Moses asked the Lord's advice, and the Lord showed him a branch. Moses took it and threw it in the water. Suddenly the water tasted sweet!

It was there at Marah that the Lord told the Israelites to listen carefully to His voice, and to obey Him. If they did this He would look after them. They wouldn't suffer from any of the terrible diseases the Egyptians had. From Marah they went to Elim, where there were 12 springs and 70 palm trees.

Often we want to do our own thing and not think about what the Lord wants us to do. God doesn't like this. He wants us to listen to Him. He tells us in the Bible exactly how to make Him happy. We need to believe in Jesus and obey Him.

Remember: Listen to Jesus' voice every day.

Manna and quail from heaven

February 8 Exodus 16

Then the Lord said to Moses, "Look, I'm going to rain down food from heaven for you. The people can go out each day and pick up as much food as they need for that day." (Exod. 16:4)

After two months the Israelites started complaining. "Oh, if only we were back in Egypt," they moaned. "At least there we had plenty to eat. But now you have brought us into this desert to die of hunger."

So the Lord promised to send them food from heaven every day. At night He sent a kind of bird, called quail. The people could catch these and eat them. Every morning, thin flakes, almost like bread, covered the ground. It was called manna. Each family had to gather just enough food for one day. If they gathered too much the leftovers went bad. On the sixth day they could gather food for two days. That was because the seventh day was the holy Sabbath, a day of rest.

It made God angry that the Israelites kept on complaining. When they moaned all the time, they showed that they didn't really believe the Lord would take care of them. The Lord wants us to be satisfied with what we have. He will make sure that we get what we need.

Remember: The Lord knows our needs.

Water from a rock

February 9 Exodus 17

The Lord said to Moses, "Take your shepherd's staff, the one you used when you struck the water of the Nile. I will meet you by the rock at Mount Horeb. Strike the rock, and water will come pouring out. Then the people will be able to drink." (Exod. 17:5-6)

The people moved on and eventually came to Rephidim. They couldn't find any water there. They grumbled and complained to Moses again. "Give us water to drink!" they demanded.

"Be quiet!" Moses said. "Why are you arguing with me? And why are you testing the Lord?" They were really testing the Lord's patience. But the people were very thirsty. They kept on grumbling. Finally Moses asked God what to do. The Lord told him to take a few of the leaders with him. They had to walk until they found a big rock at Mount Horeb. Then Moses was to strike the rock, and water would come pouring out.

Moses did exactly as he was told. When he struck the rock, fresh water gushed out. Moses gave this place two names: Massah, which means the place of testing (because they tested the Lord); and Meribah, which means the place of arguing (since this was where the people argued with Moses).

Remember: We have to do what the Lord tells us to do.

Israel beats the Amalekites

February 10 Exodus 17

As long as Moses held up the staff with his hands, the Israelites won. But as soon as he lowered his hands, the Amalekites were on the winning side. (Exod. 17:11)

While the Israelites were at Rephidim, the Amalekite army decided to fight a war against them. Moses put Joshua in charge of the Israelite soldiers. Moses watched the battle from the top of a hill. He held the staff that the Lord had given him up in the air. Aaron and a man called Hur were with Moses. As long as Moses held up the staff the Israelites were winning, but the minute he lowered his hands, the Amalekites started winning.

Eventually Moses' arms became tired, so Aaron and Hur found him a stone to sit on. Then they stood on each side of him, holding up his hands. In this way, Joshua crushed the army of Amalek.

Moses built an altar there to thank the Lord for giving them the victory. The Lord took very good care of His people. He gave them food and water and He helped them when they had to fight for their lives. The Lord still cares for His children. He takes care of us every day of our lives. If we look around us, we will see what God does for us.

Remember: Give thanks to God for everything He does.

The Israelites arrive in Sinai

February 11 Exodus 19

"Now if you will obey me and keep my covenant, you will be my own special people from among all the nations in the world. And you will be to me a kingdom that worships me every day. I will set you aside so you will be mine." (Exod. 19:5-6)

Three months after the Israelites left Egypt, they set up camp at the bottom of Mount Sinai. Moses climbed the mountain, and while he was up there the Lord told him that the Israelites would be His special people. God chose them from all the other nations on earth. They would belong to Him only. But from now on they had to do everything He told them.

Moses came down from the mountain and told the leaders of the Israelites what the Lord had said. When the Israelites heard this, they immediately said, "Of course we will do everything the Lord asks us to do."

So Moses went back up the mountain to bring the people's answer to the Lord. The Lord told Moses to tell the people to start cleaning up that very day. They had two days to wash themselves and their clothes and clean up the whole camp. On the third day, the Lord would come down to Mount Sinai. Then nobody would be allowed near the mountain.

Remember: We are special in God's eyes.

Moses goes up the mountain

February 12 Exodus 19

Moses spoke and God answered him with thunder. (Exod. 19:19)

Mount Sinai was covered with smoke because the Lord had come down to it in the form of fire. The smoke billowed into the sky and the whole mountain shook with a huge earthquake. As the horn blast grew louder and louder, Moses spoke, and God thundered His reply for everyone to hear.

The Israelites set up their camp at the bottom of Mount Sinai. At sunrise on the third day, there was a mighty thunderstorm. A thick, dark cloud came down on the mountain. A loud horn blast was heard. Moses went to the mountain to meet the Lord.

As Moses climbed up the mountain, God came down from the sky to the top of the mountain. There were giant flames all around the mountain and the whole mountain shook. The horn blasts grew louder and then the Lord's voice could be heard like thunder.

He told Moses to climb to the top. God spoke to him there. Moses had to warn the Israelites not to climb the mountain or they would die.

The Lord sent Moses to get Aaron. Then He gave them the Ten Commandments.

Remember: The Lord is God. Bow before Him.

The Ten Commandments

February 13 Exodus 20

"I am the Lord your God, who rescued you from slavery in Egypt." (Exod. 20:2)

The Lord gave Moses ten rules that the people of Israel had to obey. We call these the Ten Commandments.

The first commandment says we aren't allowed to worship any other god. We should serve only the Lord.

The second commandment says we aren't allowed to make or worship any idol. If sports, television or things like toys become more important to us than God, then they are like gods—and that is wrong.

The third commandment says we shouldn't use the name of the Lord casually. We're only allowed to use His name when we speak to the Lord and mean every word we say.

The fourth commandment says we should rest one day of the week. We Christians make Sunday our day of rest and go to church to praise the Lord together with other believers.

The fifth commandment tells us to obey our fathers and mothers. The Lord gave them to us. They have to take care of us. That is why we should love and respect them.

Remember: The Lord asks for obedience.

The Ten Commandments

February 14 Exodus 20

"Do not murder." (Exod. 20:13)

We need to obey the Ten Commandments the Lord gave the Israelites, since they are meant for all God's children.

The sixth commandment says we aren't allowed to kill anybody. Every single person's life is important to God.

The seventh commandment tells married grown-ups that they aren't allowed to fall in love with anybody except their own wife or husband. Our parents should love only each other.

The eighth commandment tells us not to steal. We shouldn't take anything that doesn't belong to us. The ninth commandment says we shouldn't lie. We always have to tell the truth, no matter how difficult it might be!

The tenth commandment tells us that we shouldn't be jealous of what others have. We shouldn't beg our parents for a new bicycle like our friend's or for new clothes and toys just because everybody else has them. The Lord tells us to be satisfied with what we have.

Remember: The things we do show what we think of God.

The golden calf

February 15 Exodus 32

When the people thought Moses was taking too long to come back down the mountain, they went to Aaron. "Look," they said, "make us some gods who can lead us. This man Moses, who brought us here from Egypt, has disappeared. We don't know what has happened to him." (Exod. 32:1)

Moses was on the mountain for quite a long time while the Lord talked to Him. God gave Moses many laws. The Israelites needed these laws so they would know what the Lord wanted them to do.

The Israelites got tired of waiting and decided to make their own god. They brought Aaron all their gold. He melted it down and made a statue that looked like a calf. The people liked it and said, "This is our god who brought us out of Egypt."

Aaron told the people that the next day there would be a festival for the Lord. The feasting started early the next morning.

The Lord was very angry about this. He told Moses to go and see what was going on. The Lord decided to destroy the Israelites, but Moses begged Him not to.

The Lord heard Moses' prayer and decided not to punish Israel with death.

Remember: The Lord hears our prayers.

Moses smashes the stone tablets

February 16 Exodus 32

When they came near the camp, Moses saw the calf and the dancing. He was so angry that he threw both stone tablets on the ground, smashing them. (Exod. 32:19)

After Moses had pleaded with the Lord to spare the lives of the Israelites, he went back down the mountain carrying two flat stones. He had written God's laws on both sides of these two stones.

As he came closer to the camp, he saw the calf and the dancing. He was so angry that he threw down the stone tablets. He grabbed the calf and threw it into the fire. When the gold had cooled, he ground it into powder and mixed it with water. He made the people drink it.

Then Moses stood at the entrance of the camp and shouted, "All of you who are on the Lord's side, come over here and join me." Everybody who didn't go over to him was killed that day. The next day Moses asked the Lord to forgive His people for sinning.

God hates sin. We shouldn't think we can get away with doing bad things just because nobody has seen us. The Lord knows everything we do.

Remember: We need to ask God to help us not to do bad things.

Moses prays for Israel

February 17 Exodus 32

Moses went to the Lord and said, "These people have done a terrible thing. They made themselves a god of gold. But now, please forgive their sin." (Exod. 32:31-32)

When Moses had punished those who were not willing to listen to the Lord, he went back up the mountain to talk to God. Moses asked Him to forgive the people's sins. Moses was willing to be punished instead. Moses said that the Lord could erase his name from the books He kept in heaven if only He would forgive the Israelites.

But the Lord refused to punish Moses in their place. He told Moses that everyone who had sinned would have to take his or her own punishment.

Moses loved the Israelites. Even though they did wicked things, he was prepared to give his life for them. He was willing to take their punishment for them. Jesus expects us to love others. He gave His life for us, so God would forgive us. We need to pray for others and help them and not think only of ourselves.

Remember: We should be kind to others.

Moses and the Lord meet in a tent

February 18 Exodus 33

Moses set up a tent far outside the camp. This was where he and the Lord met. Everyone who wanted to know the Lord's will would go there. (Exod. 33:7)

It was time for the people to move on. The Lord was still angry with them about the golden calf. He told the Israelites He would not travel along with them again.

The Israelites were sad that the Lord would not be traveling with them. They cried a lot. Then the Lord told them that He would decide what to do with them later on.

Moses put up a tent outside the camp. He said this was the tent where he spoke to the Lord. Anybody who wanted to know what the Lord thought could go there. They would tell Moses what to ask the Lord. Then Moses would go into the tent by himself. Every time he went inside, a big cloud came down over the entrance while the Lord spoke to Moses.

Whenever the people saw the cloud, they would bow low out of respect for the Lord. Inside the Tent of Meeting the Lord spoke to Moses, face to face, as someone speaks to a friend.

Remember: God speaks to us through the Bible.

The Lord travels with Israel

February 19 Exodus 33

Then Moses said, "Lord, if You don't go with us, don't let us move a step from this place. Then let us stay right here." (Exod. 33:15)

Moses remembered that the Lord had told him that He wasn't going to travel with Israel again. The people were much too sinful. So Moses asked the Lord, "Who will travel with us now?" God said, "Moses, do you want Me to come along so you can have peace?"

Then Moses answered that they weren't going anywhere without the Lord. He wasn't prepared to travel without Him. Not even an angel would be good enough to take care of them. The Lord Himself had to come along—otherwise, it would be the end of the Israelites.

Moses reminded the Lord that He had called them His special people. Surely this made them different from all the other people on earth. This was the reason the Lord should go with them. The Lord answered Moses' prayer and promised to travel with them.

The Lord is still with all His children today. We don't have to pray that the angels will guard us. We need to ask God Himself to take care of us. He is the One who protects us. He is the One at our bedside when we sleep peacefully at night, and He is the One who is there when we are afraid. All we have to do is hold His hand tightly.

Remember: The Lord keeps us safe.

The fiery cloud

February 20 Numbers 9

The day they finished setting up the tabernacle where the Lord's laws were kept, the cloud covered it. At night the cloud looked like a pillar of fire until morning. (Num. 9:15)

A while later, the Lord told Moses to make two stone tablets like the first ones. He had to climb Mount Sinai. The Lord spoke to him on top of the mountain. The Lord gave Moses the Ten Commandments again.

The Ten Commandments were kept in the tabernacle, which was a tent especially made by the best craftsmen in Israel. Bezalel and Oholiab were in charge of everybody who decorated the tabernacle. They also built an ark out of acacia wood. The cover was made of pure gold. The tablets with the Ten Commandments were placed inside the ark. When the tabernacle was finished, they dedicated it to God. A cloud covered the tabernacle, which was the sign that the Lord was there. Whenever the cloud lifted from the tabernacle, the Israelites knew it was the signal to move on. But if the cloud stayed, they would stay until it moved again. At night it looked like a column of fire.

Remember: The Lord never leaves us by ourselves.

February 21 Leviticus 1-5

The Lord wants offerings

The Lord called Moses to the tabernacle and said to him, "Give the following instructions to the Israelites: Whenever you bring offerings to the Lord, you must bring animals from your flocks and herds." (Lev. 1:1)

The Lord told the Israelites to bring Him offerings. They had to take a healthy sheep or cow or pigeon and slaughter it in front of a priest. The priest would sprinkle the blood of the animal around the altar. Then they had to burn it on the altar as a sacrifice to the Lord.

If people had sinned they could bring a guilt offering to the Lord. This was a good way of asking the Lord to forgive them for their sins. But people could also bring a thank offering to show the Lord how thankful they were to Him for being so good to them. Farmers often brought the Lord an offering of their first ripe grain or fruit. This was a way of thanking the Lord for giving them enough to eat.

Today we don't bring offerings of animals or fruit to the Lord anymore, because Jesus was sacrificed in our place. He took all our sins on Him when He died on the cross. He was punished for all we have done that is wrong, and God has forgiven us.

Remember: Jesus paid for all our sins.

The Lord gets angry if we don't listen

February 22 Leviticus 10

Moses told Aaron, "The Lord says, 'Anyone who brings Me an offering must realize I am mighty and holy. They must respect Me. I must be glorified before all the people.'" (Lev. 10:3)

One day two of Aaron's sons, Nadab and Abihu, brought the Lord an offering. But they did it in the wrong way and disobeyed the Lord's instructions. The Lord sent fire to burn them up, and they died.

Someone who brought the Lord an offering had to know exactly what to do. He had to show the Lord great respect—otherwise it was like making fun of God. Moses told Aaron this was what his sons had done. They thought they could play games with the Lord, but God will not allow that.

We should never make jokes about the Lord. Also, when we pray, we should really mean what we say. The Lord wants us to respect Him. The Lord lives in heaven. He is God. We're just ordinary people. So we need to bow down before the Lord. God makes time to listen to us. And He opens His hand full of love and gives us everything we need.

Remember: The Lord's children love Him.

The people leave Sinai

February 23 Numbers 10-11

The Lord sent a strong wind. It brought quail from the sea and let them fall into the camp and all around it! (Num. 11:31)

The people moved away from Sinai with the ark of the Lord ahead of them. Soon they started to complain again and blamed the Lord for the hard time they were having. So the Lord sent a fire in which a lot of people burned to death. Moses prayed to the Lord, and the fire stopped.

Later on the Israelites started complaining about the food. They weren't satisfied anymore with the manna the Lord sent them. They wanted meat. Moses was angry. He told the Lord he didn't want to lead the people anymore. So the Lord sent His Spirit upon 70 Israelites. They would help Moses to keep the people under control.

God also sent the Israelites the meat they asked for. Quail fell from the sky into the camp and all around it. There was more food than they could eat. But God was angry because the people were never satisfied. Lots of them died that day.

Some people are always complaining, and that is wrong. We should be satisfied with what the Lord gives us and thank Him every day for food and clothes and a place to stay.

Remember: Christians should not complain and grumble.

Twelve scouts explore Canaan

February 24 Numbers 13

The Lord said to Moses, "Send twelve men to explore the land of Canaan, the land I am giving to Israel. Send one leader from each of the twelve tribes." (Num. 13:2)

While the Israelites were in the desert of Paran, God told Moses to choose 12 men to go and explore Canaan.

After exploring the land for 40 days, the men came back. They said to Moses, "It's a great country—a land flowing with milk and honey." As proof, they showed him a branch with a bunch of grapes they had cut from a vine. It was so heavy, it took two men to carry it. But ten of the explorers were worried about the people living there: "We can't fight them. They are stronger than we are!" they said. But Caleb and Joshua didn't agree.

The ten scouts who were afraid started telling lies about the Canaanites, saying some of them were giants. This scared the Israelites so much that they wanted to stay where they were. They had already forgotten the Lord's promise to help them. Sometimes people don't have very much faith. Every time something goes wrong, they give up. We shouldn't do that!

Remember: Keep on believing! Every day!

Forty years in the desert

February 25 Numbers 14

Then the Israelites plotted among themselves, "Let's choose a new leader and go back to Egypt!" (Num. 14:4)

The Israelites didn't want to go and live in Canaan anymore. They were too scared. So they decided to choose a new leader and go back to Egypt.

Moses was shocked. He and Aaron got down on their knees and begged the people not to do this. Joshua and Caleb, two of the scouts, also told them they were making a big mistake. The Lord was on their side.

Then the Israelites started talking about stoning Joshua and Caleb. But suddenly God's glorious presence appeared above the tabernacle. Everybody saw this. The Lord told Moses He was going to destroy the Israelites. He had had enough of them!

Moses begged God to forgive them once again. The Lord answered Moses' prayer. He let the Israelites live. But God decided that not one of them would set foot in Canaan. They would wander around in the desert for 40 years. Only after they all died would their children be allowed to go into the Promised Land.

The Lord is patient with us. He keeps on giving us another chance. But we have to say we're sorry if we do something wrong, and we shouldn't do that bad thing again.

Remember: The Lord never likes to punish us.

Korah's rebellion against Moses

February 26 Numbers 16

Then Moses said to Korah and his followers, "Tomorrow morning the Lord will show us who belongs to Him and who is holy. Only those who are chosen will be allowed to come to His altar." (Num. 16:5)

One day a group of Israelites told Moses that they didn't want him to be the leader of Israel anymore. They said that the Lord had chosen them to be the new leaders.

Moses told them to come to the altar the next morning, where the people brought their offerings to the Lord. There the Lord would show who the true leaders of the people were.

The next morning, all of Israel came to see what would happen. Then they saw the mighty power of the Lord. He was furious with the people. He wanted to punish them with death, but Moses and Aaron begged Him not to punish everybody because of the sins of a few people.

So the Lord decided to punish only those who were on the side of Korah, Dathan, and Abiram. The ground suddenly opened up underneath them. The earth swallowed them up and they died.

The Lord hears us when we pray. Just think of how many times He listened when Moses prayed for the Israelites!

Remember: We shouldn't repeat bad behavior.

Buds on Aaron's staff

February 27 Numbers 17

Then the Lord said to Moses, "Take twelve wooden staffs, one from each of the twelve tribes of Israel. Write each tribal leader's name on the staff. Then put these staffs in the tabernacle in front of the ark of the covenant, where I meet with you. Buds will grow on the staff belonging to the man I choose." (Num. 17:1-5)

The morning after the deaths of Korah, Dathan, and Abiram, the people were complaining again. Once again, the Lord showed His great power at the tabernacle. He had had enough. He sent a plague, a terrible illness, which killed thousands of Israelites.

When Moses saw what was happening, he said to Aaron, "Quick, bring an offering to the Lord!" The plague ended.

Then the Lord told Moses to take 12 staffs from the leaders of the 12 tribes. They put the staffs in the tabernacle for the night. The tribe whose staff had blossoms on it the next morning would be the one chosen by the Lord to stop the rebellion.

The next morning, Aaron's staff had blossomed. This was the sign that from now on only Aaron and his sons could bring offerings to the altar of the Lord. They were to be the Lord's priests and work in the tabernacle. The Levites had to help them.

Remember: It really helps to pray for others.

The bronze snake

February 28 Numbers 21

Moses made a snake out of bronze and put it on top of a pole. When those who were bitten looked at the bronze snake, they didn't die! (Num. 21:9)

One day Aaron died. All Israel mourned his death for 30 days. Then they fought a war against Arad, king of the Canaanites. The Lord helped Israel to win the war. From there, the Israelites traveled towards the Red Sea. The people grew impatient again along the way and complained to Moses: "Why have you brought us out of Egypt to die here? There is nothing to eat here and nothing to drink. And we hate this horrible manna!"

So the Lord sent poisonous snakes, and many Israelites were bitten and died. Moses prayed again. The Lord told him to make a bronze snake and put it on top of a pole. Those who were bitten would live if they looked at it.

Just as the snake saved the lives of the Israelites in the desert, Jesus came to *our* rescue. He also was put on a wooden pole so we can live forever. If we look up at Him and believe in Him, He gives us eternal life.

Remember: The cross of Jesus brings salvation.

Balaam blesses Israel

February 29 Numbers 22

The Lord opened Balaam's eyes. Then he saw the angel of the Lord standing in the road with a drawn sword in his hand. Balaam fell face down on the ground before him. (Num. 22:31)

The Israelites won all the battles against their enemies. So when they set up camp in Moab, the people there were terrified. The Moabite king, Balak, quickly thought of something to stop them. He sent a prophet named Balaam to put a curse on Israel.

Balaam saddled his donkey and started off. But the Lord sent an angel to stand in the road and block his way. The donkey wouldn't move. Balaam couldn't see the angel, so he was angry at the donkey. Eventually the donkey lay down in the middle of the road, because it couldn't pass by the angel. Balaam hit the donkey three times. Then the Lord opened Balaam's eyes and he saw the angel.

The angel told Balaam to do exactly what the Lord told him. When Balaam met with the king, he blessed the Israelites instead of cursing them. King Balak couldn't believe his own ears. But Balaam just did what the Lord told him to do.

Remember: God changes the lives of sinners every day.

God's children should love Him

March 1 Deuteronomy 6

"Listen carefully, Israel: The Lord is our God, the Lord alone! And you must love the Lord your God with all your heart, all your soul, and all your strength." (Deut. 6:3, 5)

The Lord told the Israelites exactly how He wanted them to live. He promised they would have the land of Canaan if they obeyed Him.

The most important thing the Lord taught them was that He was the only God. They weren't allowed to worship any other god. He alone was their God and they should love Him very much. They were to think about Him every day and obey Him.

The Israelites had to talk to their children about everything the Lord told them. Every child had to be taught from the very beginning that he or she should love the Lord more than anybody else. They also had to learn to do what the Lord said. It was as if the parents were to write the Lord's laws on the hands and foreheads of their children.

Even today, mothers and fathers are expected to love the Lord. Grown-ups and children should never be too busy for the Lord. We should all learn to listen to God.

Remember: The Lord is the only God there is.

Care for those who suffer

March 2 Deuteronomy 15

"But if there are any poor people in your towns when you arrive in the land your God is giving you, do not be hardhearted or tightfisted towards them. Remember they are Israelites, the same as you. Help them!" (Deut. 15:7-8)

The Lord likes people to care for each other. That's why He told the Israelites to open their hearts and hands to those who were poor. If one Israelite saw that another Israelite was going hungry or didn't have clothes to wear, he was to help, and the Lord would bless him. God promised to take care of every person who gave to others in need. Such a person would always have plenty to live on.

God doesn't want us to believe in Him just because we want to go to heaven—although that is important. He also wants us to do good deeds for Him. We must care for each other.

We should use some of our spending money to help others and not spend it all on ourselves. We should try doing something good with it, and see what happens! The Lord will bless us once we start helping others.

Remember: We should care about our friends.

The Lord's covenant with Israel

March 3 Deuteronomy 29-30

"Today I am giving you a choice between the road of life and happiness, and the road of problems and death. Love the Lord your God and keep His laws. If you do this, you will live and become a great nation. God will bless you and the land you are about to live in." (Deut. 30:15-16)

The Lord called all the Israelites together in Moab. He said that Moses must tell them about a new agreement He was going to make with them. First the Lord reminded them how good He had been to them. He had rescued them from Egypt and helped them win many battles against other nations.

The Lord wanted Israel to be His people once more. They must have nothing to do with the gods of other nations. They had to listen only to Him, and then He would be their God forever.

Every Israelite had a choice: If he didn't want to listen to the Lord, he would die without Him. But if he obeyed Him, God would take care of him and treat him well.

The Lord doesn't force us to do what He says in the Bible. We have a choice. Of course, the Lord wants us to make the right choices. We should choose to love Him and do what is right.

Remember: We have to choose to serve the Lord every day.

The song of Moses

March 4 Deuteronomy 32

"Indeed, the Lord fights for His people. He takes care of them, because He sees that their strength is gone." (Deut. 32:36)

When Moses spoke to the Israelites about God's new covenant with them, he was already a hundred and twenty years old. He told the Israelites that he would not go into Canaan with them. The Lord had chosen a new leader in Moses' place—Joshua. Joshua had led the Israelites in wars against the kings of the Amorites, Sihon, and Og.

Moses took Joshua inside the tabernacle with him. There the Lord told Moses that the Israelites would start doing terrible things again, once he was dead. Moses had to teach the Israelites a song so that when they sang it, they would remember everything the Lord had done for them. When they sinned, the song would be a witness against them.

The song talked about how the Lord had taken Israel in His arms and protected them when He led them out of Egypt. He had shown them exactly what He wanted them to do, and they were never alone. The Lord gave His people only the best. Yet they ran after other gods. That's why He decided to punish them. But, the song said, the Lord is a merciful God who would forgive and protect them.

Remember: God cares for us and protects us.

Moses dies

March 5 Deuteronomy 33-34

Then the Lord said to Moses, "This is the land I promised to Abraham, Isaac, and Jacob. I said, 'I give this land to your descendants.' I have now allowed you to see it, but you will not set foot in it." (Deut. 34:4)

Just before he died, Moses blessed all the Israelites. He had a blessing for each of the 12 tribes of Israel. Every tribe heard that the Lord would be with them in a special way.

When Moses had finished, he started climbing Mount Nebo. From one of the mountain peaks, the Lord showed him the land where the Israelites were going to live. The Lord told Moses this was the land He had promised to Abraham, Isaac, and Jacob a long time ago.

Moses died all alone on the mountain. The Lord buried him. The Israelites mourned Moses' death for 30 days.

The Lord used Moses in a wonderful way. He loved the Lord very much and he loved the Israelites, even though they caused lots of trouble. He prayed for them often and asked God not to punish them.

If we love God, we will obey Him, care for others, and pray to Him.

Remember: We should pray for our friends every day.

Joshua: God's new hero

March 6 Joshua 1

"Be strong and courageous! Do not be afraid or discouraged. I, the Lord your God, am with you wherever you go." (Josh. 1:9)

Joshua took over after Moses' death. He had to lead the Israelites across the Jordan River into the Promised Land. The Lord talked to him before he started on the journey. He told Joshua that He would be with him all the time. What a wonderful promise! But Joshua had to keep every word of the Lord locked away in his heart, and do what he was told. He had to walk in the ways of the Lord every minute of every day.

The Lord also told Joshua never to be afraid. He had a very difficult job. He had to lead a large nation into a new country, and the people could be very difficult at times. They didn't always listen to the Lord, but Joshua knew that God would help him every step of the way.

The Lord wants us to be brave, like Joshua. We don't need to be afraid when the Lord is with us. The most powerful Person in the whole world is on our side and is there to look after us!

Remember: The Lord is always with us.

Two spies go to Jericho

March 7 Joshua 2

Then Joshua secretly sent out two spies from the Israelite camp. He told them, "Spy out the land of Canaan, especially the city of Jericho." (Josh. 2:1)

Joshua decided to send two spies to Canaan. He especially wanted to know how strong the city of Jericho was.

In Jericho the two men stayed at the house of a woman called Rahab. She had a very bad reputation. Someone saw the men there and told the king. He sent soldiers to Rahab's house to look for them, but Rahab hid them and told the king's men they had already left the city.

When the soldiers had gone, Rahab begged the two men to ask the Israelites to let her and her family live when they attacked Jericho. They promised to do this. Rahab's house was built into the city wall, and the men were able to climb down the wall on a rope.

Before the two men left, they told Rahab to leave the scarlet rope hanging from her window. Then they could guarantee her safety when they attacked the city.

The two men went back to Joshua and told him, "The Lord will definitely give us the land. Everybody there is terrified of us."

Remember: No problem is too big for God.

Twelve stones

March 8 Joshua 3-4

So the men did as Joshua told them. They took twelve stones from the middle of the Jordan River, one for each tribe, just as the Lord had told Joshua. They carried them to the place where they camped for the night. (Josh. 4:8)

Joshua and the Israelites got ready to cross the Jordan River. Joshua told the priests to lift up the ark of the covenant and lead the people across the river.

As the feet of the priests touched the water, the Lord stopped the flow of the water. The priests carrying the ark stood in the middle of the river on dry ground, while the Israelites crossed over.

When all the people were safely across the river, the Lord told Joshua to call the 12 leaders, one from each of the tribes of Israel. They each had to pick up one stone from the Jordan River and take it with them. Later, they used these stones to build a memorial at the place they camped for the night. This was to remind them and their children that the Lord had helped them cross the Jordan River without getting wet. As soon as the priests walked out on the other side of the Jordan, the water flowed again.

Remember: The Lord still does miracles today.

Jericho is destroyed

March 9 Joshua 6

When the Israelite soldiers heard the sound of the horns, they shouted as loud as they could. Suddenly, the walls of Jericho collapsed. And the Israelites took the city. (Josh. 6:20)

The people of Jericho knew the Israelites were going to attack, so they locked all the gates of the city. Joshua told the priests to march around the city once a day for six days, carrying the ark of the covenant. Israel's army marched with them, some in front and others behind them. Joshua told them, "Don't say a single word until I tell you to shout. Then shout!"

On the seventh day, the Israelites marched around the city seven times. The seventh time around, as the priests sounded their horns, Joshua gave the command: "Shout!" The walls of Jericho collapsed. The soldiers charged into the city and killed everybody except Rahab and her family. The soldiers took all the gold and silver for God.

The Lord gave the Israelites a great victory. He is so strong that He can do anything.

Remember: Our God is a great God.

Achan's sin

March 10 Joshua 7

The Israelites had to give the Lord all the gold and silver they took from Jericho. But some of them kept it for themselves. A man named Achan stole some of these things, so the Lord was very angry with the Israelites. (Josh. 7:1)

Joshua sent some of his warriors to attack Ai. But the army of Ai defeated the Israelites.

Joshua was upset and wanted to know why they lost when the Lord had promised to help them. God told Joshua it was because the Israelites were disobedient. They had taken some of the gold and silver for themselves instead of giving it to Him.

The next morning, Joshua called all the Israelites together. The Lord identified Achan as the guilty one. Achan admitted that he had taken five pounds of silver and a pound of gold when they captured Jericho. He had also helped himself to some clothing and had buried everything under his tent.

Joshua told Achan it was his fault that a lot of soldiers had lost their lives in the battle against Ai. Because Achan had brought trouble to the Israelites, he and his family were punished.

Remember: The Lord sees everything we do.

Ai is defeated

March 11 Joshua 8

Then the Lord said to Joshua, "Do not be afraid or discouraged. Take your whole army and attack Ai. I will give you the king of Ai, his people, his city, and his land." (Josh. 8:1)

After the death of Achan and his family, the Lord told Joshua to attack Ai again. This time they would win. Joshua made a clever plan. He hid thirty thousand men close behind the city and told them to be ready for action. Then he and the rest of the army attacked Ai from the other side. The king of Ai and his soldiers fought back. Joshua and his men pretended to be losing and retreated. The army of Ai went after them, leaving the city unprotected. The soldiers, who had been hiding, took the city and burned it down. Joshua and his men then turned to face the king of Ai and his army and defeated them.

Joshua built an altar on Mount Ebal to thank the Lord for giving them the victory. He read the law of the Lord to all the Israelites, reminding them to obey God.

Remember: We should be glad that the Lord cares for us.

The sun and the moon stand still

March 12 Joshua 10

On the day the Lord helped Israel win the battle against the Amorites, Joshua prayed to the Lord in front of all the people of Israel. He said, "Sun, stand still over Gibeon. Moon, stand still over the valley of Aijalon." (Josh. 10:12)

The five Amorite kings were very angry when they heard that the Gibeonites had made peace with Israel. They decided to attack the city of Gibeon. The Gibeonites immediately asked Joshua for help.

The Lord told Joshua He would give the Israelites victory over the Amorites, and He did. At one point, Joshua asked the Lord to make the sun stand still so that they could finish the battle. The miracle happened—the sun stood still. Never before had anything like this happened.

The Lord is so powerful that even the sun listens to Him. If the Lord wants to, He can bring the whole world to a standstill. He has the sun and the moon and the stars in the palm of His hand. He will also do great things for us if we ask Him.

Remember: The Lord does wonderful things for His children.

Joshua asks Israel to serve the Lord

March 13 Joshua 24

"If you are not willing to serve the Lord, then choose today whom you will serve. Would you prefer the gods your ancestors served? Or will it be the gods of the Amorites, in whose land you now live? But as for me and my family, we will serve the Lord." (Josh. 24:15)

Joshua won one battle after the other against the Canaanite kings. He defeated 31 kings. Later on he took the whole land of Canaan and divided it between the 12 tribes of Israel.

At the end of his life, Joshua called the Israelite leaders together. He told the people how good the Lord had been to them. Then he told them to choose who they wanted to serve. They could either serve the Lord or the gods of the land where they now lived. But no matter what they decided, he and his family would always be faithful to the Lord.

The people answered, all together, "We would never turn our backs on the Lord and worship other gods." But Joshua wasn't satisfied. "The Lord is a holy God. He won't allow people to serve Him just when it suits them." But the Israelites promised again to serve the Lord.

Remember: We should love the Lord with all our heart!

March 14 Judges 2

The Israelites do not obey God

While Joshua was alive the Israelites served the Lord. After he and all the people of his time died, another generation grew up who did not know the Lord. They didn't know about the mighty things He had done for Israel. (Judg. 2:7, 10)

While Joshua was alive, the Israelites obeyed the Lord. But after his death it was a different story. The next generation grew up knowing nothing about the Lord. The Israelites turned their backs on the Lord and started worshiping the gods of their new country.

The sins of Israel made the Lord very angry. They had forgotten all the promises the Lord had made to their fathers and grandfathers.

How can we make sure that we grow up knowing about the Lord? We need to read the Bible and go to church every Sunday. If we don't love the Lord when we are little, we are going to grow up without Him—and nothing can be worse than that.

Remember: We need to read the Bible and go to church every Sunday.

The Lord sends judges

March 15 Judges 3

The Israelites cried out to the Lord for help. Then He sent a man to rescue them. His name was Othniel, the son of Caleb's younger brother, Kenaz. The Spirit of the Lord was with him. He ruled over Israel. (Judg. 3:9-10)

Because the Israelites were very sinful, the Lord allowed a Mesopotamian king to have control over them for eight years. Then the Israelites started praying. The Lord heard their prayers, and He sent a judge to rule over them. He was called Othniel. He fought a war against the king of Mesopotamia and won. As long as Othniel lived, there was peace in Israel.

After Othniel's death, Israel lost a war against King Eglon of Moab. They worked for him for 18 years. Then the Israelites started praying again, and the Lord sent Ehud to their rescue.

Ehud arranged to meet with King Eglon alone. As soon as the servants had been sent out of the room, Ehud pulled out his dagger and killed the king. He gathered the Israelites together, and they attacked and defeated the Moabites.

The Lord notices when people suffer, even if they are sinners.

Remember: The Lord never sleeps or rests.

Deborah and Barak

March 16 Judges 4

The Israelites cried out to the Lord for help. At that time, Deborah, the wife of Lappidoth, was the leader of the Israelites. (Judg. 4:3-4)

After Ehud's death, the Israelites started doing evil things again. So the Lord let King Jabin, the Canaanite king who lived in Hazor, rule over them. Sisera was in charge of his army.

During that time, a woman was the leader of Israel. Her name was Deborah. One day, the Lord told her that Israel would win the battle against Sisera. She sent for Barak to lead Israel's army. Barak said, "I will go, but only if you go with me!" "Very well," she replied, "I will go with you, but the victory will be the Lord's, not yours."

Israel's ten thousand soldiers defeated Sisera's army that day. Sisera tried to escape and hid in the tent of a woman called Jael. He was very tired. When he was fast asleep Jael killed him. She called Barak to show him that Sisera was dead. That same day, Barak captured King Jabin. The Canaanites were defeated.

After Israel's great victory, Deborah and Barak sang a song and praised the Lord. They were very happy that the Lord had helped them. We can't do anything without the Lord.

Remember: The Lord helps His children when times are hard.

God calls Gideon

March 17 Judges 6

Gideon said to God, "I will put a piece of sheep's wool on the ground tonight. If it is wet with dew in the morning but the ground around it is dry, then I will know that You are going to help me rescue Israel as You promised." (Judg. 6:36-37)

After a while, the Lord let the Midianites take control of the Israelites. So, the Israelites prayed for help again. God sent an angel to a man called Gideon.

Gideon hurried home to get an offering for the Lord. The angel told him to put it down on a rock. Suddenly, fire blazed up from the rock and burned the offering. Gideon realized that the Lord was there with him.

To make sure God really wanted him to rescue Israel, Gideon asked the Lord to give him a sign. He would leave a piece of sheep's wool outside that night. If the wool was wet the next morning, and the ground around it was quite dry, then he would know that this was what he must do. It happened just that way, but Gideon still wasn't sure. He said to God, "Please don't be angry with me, but this time let the wool stay dry, and the ground around it be wet." The next morning it had happened just like that, so Gideon knew what he had to do.

Remember: Only ask God for good things.

March 18 Judges 7

Gideon defeats the Midianites

The Lord told Gideon, "With these three hundred men I will rescue you and give you victory over the Midianites." (Judg. 7:7)

Gideon and his men prepared to fight a war against the Midianites. God told him he had too many warriors, so Gideon sent home twenty-two thousand men who admitted they were scared. That left ten thousand soldiers—still too many. So the Lord sent them to the river to drink water. Only three hundred men drank the water from their cupped hands. Only these men were chosen to be Gideon's army.

Gideon divided his men into three groups. He gave each man a ram's horn and a clay jar with a torch in it. That night they went to the Midianite camp. Suddenly, they blew their horns and broke their jars. They held the blazing torches in the air and shouted, "A sword for the Lord and for Gideon!"

The Midianites panicked and started rushing around. Some of them even fought against each other in the confusion.

The Lord used three hundred warriors to defeat a powerful army. It doesn't matter how strong or smart we are. God uses ordinary people. We don't even have to wait until we are grown-ups. God will use us just the way we are, if we give our lives to Him.

Remember: One believer can make a difference.

Samson, the strong man

March 19 Judges 13

"One of these days you will have a son. His hair must never be cut, because he will belong to God from birth. He will rescue Israel from the Philistines." (Judg. 13:5)

The Philistines oppressed the Israelites for 40 years. During that time, the Lord sent an angel to a woman in Israel. He told her she would have a son. He would be special, because he would help Israel against the Philistines. Samson was not allowed to drink any wine or beer or have his hair cut.

The woman told her husband, Manoah, about the angel's visit. Manoah prayed that the angel would come back and tell them exactly what the Lord wanted them to do.

The angel came back later. After he had told them how to raise the boy, Manoah prepared an offering for the Lord. Then the Lord did something amazing. Flames from the altar shot up toward the sky, and the angel of the Lord went up to heaven in the flame.

When the baby boy was born, his parents called him Samson, and the Spirit of the Lord was with him.

Remember: The Lord always cares about children.

Samson's riddle

March 20 Judges 14

"What is sweeter than honey? What is stronger than a lion?" (Judg. 14:18)

Samson decided to marry a Philistine girl who lived in Timnah. One day, when he was on his way there, a lion attacked him, but the Lord helped him to kill the lion. Later, when Samson went back to Timnah for the wedding, he saw that a swarm of bees had made some honey in the carcass of the lion.

Samson threw a party at Timnah and invited 30 Philistine men. He said, "Let me tell you a riddle: From the one who eats came something to eat; out of the strong came something sweet." He promised to give each of the Philistines a set of clothes if they could solve the riddle within seven days. If they failed, they each had to give him a set of clothes.

Three days later, they were still trying to figure it out. Then they told his wife to get the answer from Samson. She nagged Samson until he told her: "What is sweeter than honey? What is stronger than a lion?"

On the seventh day, the Philistines brought Samson the answer. He went to Ashkelon where he killed 30 men and gave their clothes to the others. Then he left his wife and went back home to his parents.

Remember: We should choose our friends carefully.

Samson fights the Philistines

March 21 Judges 15

Then he picked up a donkey's jawbone that was lying on the ground and killed a thousand Philistines with it. (Judg. 15:15)

Some time after this, Samson decided to visit his wife in Timnah again. He discovered that her father had given her to another man in the meantime. He told Samson to marry her sister. This made Samson so angry that he went out and caught three hundred foxes. He tied their tails together in pairs and fastened a torch to each pair of tails. Then he chased the foxes through the fields of the Philistines. Everything was burned down.

The Philistines wanted to kill Samson for what he'd done, but they couldn't find him. So, they attacked the Israelites, thinking he was among them. The Israelites caught Samson, tied him up, and took him to the Philistines. But Samson snapped the ropes on his arms. He picked up a donkey's jawbone that was lying on the ground and killed a thousand Philistines with it.

The Lord gave Samson this great strength. He used it to help the Israelites against their enemies.

Remember: God is always there to help us.

Samson and Delilah

March 22 Judges 16

Then Samson prayed to the Lord, "O God, please make me strong again, just this once, so that I may pay back the Philistines for blinding me." (Judg. 16:28)

Samson fell in love with a Philistine woman named Delilah. The leaders of the Philistines went to her secretly. "Find out from Samson what makes him so strong," they said.

Delilah kept asking Samson what made him so strong. Every time she asked, he gave her a different reason. In the end, after Delilah went on nagging him, he told her the truth. If his hair was cut, his strength would go. When he fell asleep, Delilah had his hair shaved off. Then the Philistines came, put him in chains, and blinded him.

Samson's hair started growing again in the Philistine prison. One day, the Philistines held a festival in the temple of the god Dagon. Samson was brought out to perform for them. As he stood between the two pillars that held up the roof of the temple, he prayed that the Lord would give him back his strength one more time. He put his arms around the two pillars and pushed against them with all his might. The temple crashed down on the people. Samson died with them that day.

Remember: The Lord can do anything.

Naomi and Ruth

March 23 Ruth 1-2

Ruth said to Naomi, "Don't ask me to leave you and turn back. I will go wherever you go and live wherever you live. Your people will be my people, and your God will be my God." (Ruth 1:16)

There was a famine in Israel, so a man called Elimelech and his wife, Naomi, decided to move to Moab with their two sons. The sons married Moabite girls called Ruth and Orpah. Elimelech died, and then his sons did as well.

Naomi decided to go back to Bethlehem. Her two daughters-in-law wanted to go with her, but she told them it would be better for them to stay in Moab. Orpah turned back, but Ruth refused to go. She went to Bethlehem with Naomi and said she wanted to serve God and be an Israelite.

In Bethlehem, Ruth picked up leftover grain in the fields of a man called Boaz. When Boaz saw Ruth gathering the grain, he told the harvesters to drop some heads of barley on purpose for her to take home. Naomi was very thankful. She said the Lord would bless Boaz.

Sometimes life is hard. But the Lord always has a plan for the lives of His children. Even if we suffer, we must never stop believing.

Remember: Care about those who suffer.

March 24 Ruth 4

Ruth and Boaz get married

So Boaz married Ruth ... (Ruth 4:13)

Naomi told her daughter-in-law Ruth to go to Boaz and ask him to help her. So, one evening, she went to the threshing floor where Boaz was lying fast asleep. Ruth lay down at his feet. When he woke up, she asked him to help and protect her.

Later, after Ruth had gone home, Boaz asked the leaders of the town for advice. He wanted to buy Naomi's land in order to help Ruth and Naomi. First, Boaz asked a relative of Naomi's if he wanted to buy the land, but he wasn't interested. So, Boaz went ahead.

Soon afterwards, Boaz married Ruth. They had a son named Obed. Everybody was happy that the Lord had been so good to Ruth and Naomi.

The Lord loves all His children. He will lead us along the right path if we ask Him. Sometimes it takes a long time for His plans for our lives to work out, but we should always trust Him.

Remember: The Lord is always good to us.

Hannah's promise to the Lord

March 25 1 Samuel 1

"In that case," Eli said to Hannah, "Cheer up! May the God of Israel give you what you have asked of Him." "Oh, thank you, sir!" she exclaimed. (1 Sam. 1:17-18)

A man named Elkanah had two wives, Peninnah and Hannah. Peninnah had children, while Hannah did not.

Every year, Elkanah and his wives would travel to Shiloh to worship and sacrifice to the Lord. All the women there would make fun of Hannah, because she was childless.

One day, Hannah went to the temple in Shiloh to pray. She asked the Lord to give her a son. If He did, she would give the boy back to Him.

While she was praying, Eli the priest watched her. He saw her lips move, but she made no sound. He thought she was drunk. "Oh, no sir!" she said to him, "I'm not drunk! But I am very sad, and I was pouring out my heart to the Lord." Eli told her that God would answer her prayer. She could go back home.

The next day, Hannah went back home with her husband. She was not worried anymore. She believed that the Lord had heard her prayer.

Remember: Every child is a gift from God.

Samuel hears the Lord's voice

March 26 1 Samuel 3

Meanwhile, the boy Samuel worked for the Lord by helping Eli in the temple. In those days, messages from the Lord were very rare. (1 Sam. 3:1)

God answered Hannah's prayer for a son. She had a child and named him Samuel. When Samuel was old enough, she took him to Eli the priest in Shiloh as she had promised the Lord. Samuel worked in the temple. Every year, Hannah visited him. The Lord gave her five more children.

One night, Samuel was asleep in the temple near the ark of God. Suddenly, the Lord called, "Samuel! Samuel!" The boy thought it was Eli. But Eli said he hadn't called him and Samuel should go back to bed. It happened a second time. When it happened the third time, Eli realized it was the Lord calling Samuel. So Eli told Samuel that, if he heard the voice again, he should say, "Yes, Lord, your servant is listening."

The Lord then told Samuel that He was going to punish Eli and his family. Eli's sons were bad, and Eli didn't discipline them. When Eli wanted to know what the Lord had said, Samuel told him. Eli answered, "It is the Lord's will. Let Him do what He thinks best."

Remember: The Lord also uses children in His service.

The Philistines steal the ark of the Lord

March 27 1 Samuel 3-4

As Samuel grew up, the Lord was with him, and everything Samuel said was wise and helpful. All the people of Israel knew that Samuel was truly a prophet of the Lord. (1 Sam. 3:19-20)

Samuel grew up, and the Lord was with him. Samuel brought all the messages the Lord gave him to the people.

At the time, Israel was fighting a war with the Philistines. They defeated the Israelite army, so the soldiers of Israel decided to get the Lord's ark in Shiloh. Eli's sons, Hophni and Phinehas, helped carry the ark to where the battle was being fought. When the ark arrived at their camp, the soldiers started shouting with joy.

When the Philistines heard all the shouting, they began to panic. "Their God has come into their camp!" they cried. "Fight as you never have before!" That day, the Philistines killed thirty thousand Israelites and took the ark. Eli's sons were killed.

Others must see that we belong to the Lord. We need to listen to what the Lord teaches us in the Bible. Then our friends will notice that we have a special Friend on our side. We shouldn't be embarrassed to talk about Him.

Remember: People can see if we serve the Lord.

The Philistines send the ark back

March 28 1 Samuel 5-6

The Philistines carried the ark of God into the temple of Dagon and placed it beside the idol of Dagon. But when the citizens of Ashdod went to see it the next morning, Dagon had fallen with his face to the ground in front of the ark of the Lord! (1 Sam. 5:2-3)

The Philistines took the ark of God to a city named Ashdod. There, they put it in the temple of Dagon, one of their gods. The next morning, when they went into the temple, they found the idol of Dagon face down on the ground. The next day, the same thing happened.

After this, the people of Ashdod started getting sick. So they sent the ark to a place called Gath. Everybody there also got sick. From there, the ark was sent to Ekron. The same thing happened there, so the Philistines decided to send the ark back to the Israelites.

The Philistines sent gifts of gold along with the ark. When the ark arrived at Beth-shemesh in Israel, some of the people were curious and peeked into the ark. Seventy of them died. So the people offered guilt offerings to the Lord. Then they sent the ark to a place called Kiriat-jearim. It stayed there in the house of Abinadab for 20 years. Abinadab's son Eleazar was in charge of the ark, and there was peace in Israel again.

Remember: The Lord does not allow people to mock Him.

The Israelites want a king

March 29 1 Samuel 8

All the leaders of Israel met at Ramah to discuss the matter with Samuel. "Look," they told him, "you are now old, and your sons are not like you. Give us a king like all the other nations have." (1 Sam. 8:4-5)

Samuel's two sons weren't like their father. They took bribes, and they didn't serve the Lord. The leaders of Israel were worried about this, because Samuel was already very old.

So the leaders asked Samuel to give them a king. Samuel didn't want to. He asked the Lord's advice. The Lord said, "Do as they say and give them a king." He knew they wouldn't listen to Samuel's warnings anyway. The big mistake the people made was to think that the Lord was not good enough to be their king anymore.

So, Samuel told the people they could have a king, but he warned them about how a king would treat them. Many Israelites would have to work for the king. They would also have to pay taxes. By the time they started complaining, it would be too late, and the Lord would not listen.

But the Israelites refused to change their minds. "Even so, we still want a king," they said.

Remember: We need to listen to what the Lord says in the Bible.

Saul, the first king of Israel

March 30 1 Samuel 9-10

When Samuel noticed Saul, the Lord said, "That's the man I told you about! He will rule my people." (1 Sam. 9:17)

One day, a man from the tribe of Benjamin went to look for his father's donkeys. His name was Saul. He couldn't find the donkeys anywhere. His servant told him about Samuel. Maybe he could help them. So, they went to the town where Samuel was.

Now, the Lord had told Samuel the day before that He would send someone to him. Samuel had to anoint him as the new king of Israel. When Samuel saw Saul, the Lord said, "This is the man!"

Later, after they had eaten, Saul set out to go home. He and Samuel left the house together. Outside the town, Samuel anointed Saul as king. That day, the Spirit of the Lord came upon Saul. Everybody could see the Lord was working through him.

Later, Samuel called the people together at Mizpah. He told them that God had chosen Saul to be their first king. All the people shouted, "Long live the king!"

The Lord does great things! Today, He still gives His Spirit to everyone who bows before Him. The Holy Spirit will live in us too if we love the Lord. He shows us the right way and helps us to love God.

Remember: God wants us to live for Him every day.

Saul defeats the Ammonites

March 31 1 Samuel 11

But Saul replied, "No one will be killed today, for today the Lord has rescued Israel!" (1 Sam. 11:13)

The Ammonite king attacked an Israelite city called Jabesh. His soldiers surrounded the city. The citizens of Jabesh promised to be the king's servants if he would let them live. The king said, "All right, but only on one condition. Only if I can hurt everybody!"

Messengers went to Saul in Gibeah and told him what the Ammonite king wanted to do. The Spirit of the Lord made Saul become very angry. He took two oxen and cut them into pieces. He sent the pieces throughout Israel with the message: "This is what will happen to the oxen of anyone who refuses to follow Samuel and Saul into battle!" Then, Saul attacked the Ammonites. Saul's army won the battle and saved the people of Jabesh. The soldiers were very happy about winning. They wanted to kill everyone who was against having Saul as king. But Saul stopped them. The Lord had helped them to win. No Israelite would be killed.

Then Saul went to Gilgal. There, before the Lord, the people crowned him king. Saul and all the Israelites were very happy.

Remember: Praise the Lord for His love.

April 1 1 Samuel 12

Samuel talks to the Israelites

"Don't be afraid," Samuel said. "You have done wrong to ask for a king, but make sure now that you worship the Lord with all your heart." (1 Sam. 12:20)

One day, Samuel spoke to the Israelites again. He said he had always told them what the Lord wanted. He also told them it was wrong to ask for a king. But the Lord would not hold this against them. If the Israelites and their king worshiped the Lord and listened to His voice, all would be well. But if they didn't, there would be hard times ahead for them.

Then Samuel prayed. Suddenly, the Lord sent thunder and rain. All the people were terrified of the Lord and of Samuel.

"Pray to the Lord your God for us, or we will die!" they cried.

Samuel told them not to be afraid. They just had to hold on to the Lord's hand, and He would be with them.

The Lord is mighty and important. If He tells us to listen, then we must listen. It's the best thing we can ever do, because it pleases the most powerful Person in the whole world. Just think, it's possible for us—ordinary, puny little people—to make the Lord happy!

Remember: The most important Person in the world is with us.

Saul sins

April 2 1 Samuel 13

Samuel said to Saul, "You have done a foolish thing. Why have you offered the burnt offering yourself? You have disobeyed the command of the Lord your God. If you had obeyed, you would have been king over Israel for the rest of your life. But now you will not be king much longer. The Lord has chosen a man after His own heart." (1 Sam. 13:13-14)

One day, the Philistines declared war against the Israelites. The men of Israel got scared and ran away. King Saul and his soldiers were still in Gilgal waiting for Samuel to bring an offering to the Lord before they went to fight against the Philistines.

When Samuel took too long to come, Saul decided to offer the burnt offering himself. Just then, Samuel arrived. He was very angry with Saul. He told Saul he had made a big mistake. He had offered the burnt offering himself even though he knew that only Samuel was allowed to do it. Because of what he had done, the Lord would take his kingship away from him.

We shouldn't think we're always right. We should listen to our parents and to what they tell us about God.

Remember: We must obey our parents' teachings about God.

April 3 1 Samuel 16

God chooses David as king

God's Spirit made David strong. (1 Sam. 16:13)

King Saul didn't do what the Lord asked him to do. This upset the Lord, and He decided to choose another king. He knew that one of Jesse's sons would make a good king.

The Lord sent Samuel to show everybody who the new king would be. Jesse called his sons and wondered which one the Lord would choose. As each son came before Samuel, the old prophet shook his head and said, "No, not this one." When Samuel had seen all of Jesse's sons, he said, "The Lord has not chosen any of these. Don't you have any other sons?" "There's the youngest," Jesse answered. "But he's out in the fields watching the sheep." Surely it couldn't be him! Then Samuel said to Jesse, "It's not important to the Lord what a person is like on the outside. It's the heart that counts."

So Jesse sent for David. When David walked in, Samuel knew he was the king that the Lord had chosen, and he told the others that David was their new king. From then on, the Holy Spirit worked in David in a very special way. He made David strong so that he could be a good king someday.

Remember: God looks into our hearts to see if they are clean.

God watches over David

April 4 Psalm 23

The Lord is my shepherd. (Ps. 23:1)

David was a shepherd, and he took care of his sheep. He was often alone in the fields with them, but he was not afraid. He knew the Lord was always with him. In a beautiful poem (Ps. 23) he tells us why he was never afraid.

This is what he says:

"The Lord is like a shepherd to me. I am like His sheep. He takes good care of me. He gives me everything I need. When I'm tired, He lets me rest like a sheep rests on soft, green grass. When I'm thirsty, He gives me cool water. So I don't need to worry about anything.

"When He is with me, I feel safe. I can handle anything. When I don't know the right thing to do, He helps me. He leads me in the right ways. Even if I feel I'm all alone in the darkest night, I'm not scared, because the Lord is with me. He comforts me. With Him, I am safe."

The Lord takes good care of His children. If we believe in Him, we don't ever have to be afraid. He will watch over us just like a good shepherd watches over his sheep.

Remember: God Himself takes care of us.

David does his duty

April 5 1 Samuel 16

"I heard the boy, David, play the harp. The Lord is with him." (1 Sam. 16:18)

David was only a shepherd boy, but the Lord, who loved him very much, chose David to become king. God's plan was for David to be King Saul's helper in the palace at first so that he could learn how things were done before he became king.

David was a very talented harp player. When King Saul was tired or upset, David would play the harp. It made the king feel better and calmed him down. All the other tasks he had to do for the king, David did well. He worked hard because he loved God very much and obeyed Him. David knew it would hurt God if he did something wrong, and he knew that the Lord was helping him every day.

David wrote a poem about God Who always helps His children.
He says in Psalm 27:
"The Lord is the one who always helps me. So why should I be afraid? I can always go to Him. I know the Lord will help me. That's why I feel strong, because I put my trust in the Lord."

Remember: We can always go to the Lord.

A shepherd believes and wins

April 6 1 Samuel 17

"All right, go ahead. And may the Lord be with you." (1 Sam. 17:37)

David wasn't afraid. One day, as he was watching his father's sheep, a vicious lion snatched one of David's lambs. David didn't run away. He went after the lion and killed him and took the lamb from the lion's mouth. He also killed a bear once.

David was very brave. One day, David's father asked him to take his brothers something to eat. There was a war going on, and they were soldiers. When David arrived with the food, he heard Goliath the giant making fun of the Israelites. Everybody was too scared to fight the giant.

David told the king he wasn't afraid of Goliath. He would fight him. At first, the king wasn't happy about this. Goliath had been a soldier for many years. David was only a shepherd boy. But David said to him, "Don't worry about a thing. The Lord helped me to kill the lion and the bear. He will also help me win the fight against Goliath."

"All right, go ahead," King Saul said. "And may the Lord be with you." And the Lord did help David!

Remember: Trust the Lord!

Goliath

April 7 1 Samuel 17

"You come to me with sword, spear, and javelin, but I come to you in the name of the Lord Almighty." (1 Sam. 17:45)

The Philistines were the enemies of God's people. They fought wars against them. The Philistines had a very strong man on their side whose name was Goliath. He was a giant and a very good fighter. Everybody was terrified of him. He made fun of the Israelites, because their God couldn't even help them against him. He was too strong. But he soon found out that he was wrong.

David loved God, and God loved him. He knew God would help him, so he wasn't afraid of Goliath. David put his slingshot and five smooth stones in his pocket. When Goliath saw this young boy, who was not even armed for battle, he was furious. He thought they were joking. He started swearing and shouted, "Come over here, and I'll fight you."

David walked towards him and, with one stone, hit him between the eyes. Goliath the giant fell down dead. The Philistines were terrified. They turned and ran off in all directions. They realized that God is stronger than any human being.

Remember: God is stronger than any human being.

God watches over David and saves him from Saul

April 8 1 Samuel 18-19

Saul was afraid of David, because the Lord helped him. (1 Sam. 18:12)

King Saul soon noticed that David was very popular with the people. The Lord was very good to David. Saul became jealous of David. Saul didn't always listen to the Lord. He was disobedient. Sometimes, he acted as if the Devil was in him.

One day, when David was playing the harp for Saul, Saul hurled a spear at him. David ducked, and the spear missed him. Then Saul chased David away from the palace. He decided to kill David.

Another time, Saul sent soldiers to capture David. They knew he was with his wife Michal. But Michal warned David, and she thought of a clever plan to save him. She put a rope out of the window, and he climbed down it and ran away. Then Michal made the bed so it looked like David was in it. She told the soldiers that David was sick. It gave David a chance to get away. By the time the soldiers realized they had been fooled, it was already too late. Once again, the Lord had protected David.

Remember: The Lord protects His children.

David and Jonathan

April 9 1 Samuel 20

Go in peace. (1 Sam. 20:42)

David and King Saul's son Jonathan were best friends, but Saul was jealous of David and wanted him dead. David had to hide. He told Jonathan he needed his help. He wanted Jonathan to find out if Saul was really serious about killing him. Jonathan arranged a special signal with David to give him the answer. He would shoot an arrow at a target. David had to hide nearby. If Jonathan said to his helper, "The arrow is close, on this side," David would know he was safe. But if Jonathan said, "The arrow is over there, on the far side," David would know Saul was going to kill him.

Jonathan asked Saul if he was determined to kill David. "Yes, of course," Saul answered. Jonathan went off with his bow and shot an arrow. "The arrow is over there, farther on," he called out loudly to his helper. This was the sign for David to run for his life. Jonathan was sad that he would never see his friend again, but he knew he had to help save his life.

We must do what's best for our friends, even if it sometimes hurts.

Remember: Always do the right thing, even if it sometimes hurts.

David spares Saul's life

April 10 1 Samuel 24

Saul said to David, "You are a better man than I am." (1 Sam. 24:18)

The Lord took good care of David, and He helped him. This made King Saul very jealous. He gave orders to his soldiers to find David and kill him. Saul went along to search for David. They traveled a long way in the hot sun, and after awhile they were very tired. At a cave, Saul decided to rest for a little while. He didn't know that David was hiding in the cave. Saul lay down and fell asleep. David went up to him quietly and cut off a piece of Saul's clothing. David's men wanted him to kill Saul. "This is your chance," they whispered. But David refused. He didn't want to do anything that would not please the Lord.

When Saul woke up, David showed him the piece of cloth. "I would never harm you, my king," David said. Saul saw that David could have killed him but didn't. This made him sad, and he cried. He was so mean to David, yet David did not try to pay him back.

Then Saul knew that the Lord doesn't want us to hurt others, no matter how jealous we are.

Remember: Never hurt other people.

April 11 Psalm 1

Choose your friends carefully

It is good not to listen to the wrong advice. (Ps. 1:1)

The wrong friends can make us do wicked things. They often try to get us to do something that we know is wrong. Psalm 1 tells us about this.

We shouldn't listen to bad friends. We should ignore them when they tell us to be naughty, because doing wrong makes God unhappy.

We can think of it like this: A tree is planted beside a beautiful stream. Its leaves are a shiny green, and its fruit is good. Someone who listens to the Lord is like this tree. Someone who doesn't listen to the Lord is like a handful of dried-up leaves blown away by the wind. One day, the Lord will punish people who don't love Him. The Lord tells His children what they must do, but wicked people don't listen to Him. Psalm 1:6 says: "Truly, the Lord walks alongside the person who listens to Him."

If we listen to Him, we are like a lovely green tree with delicious fruit. We please the Lord and make Him proud of us.

Remember: We shouldn't listen to bad friends.

David becomes king

April 12 1 Chronicles 11

The Lord, who is the most powerful of all, was with David. (1 Chron. 11:9)

Remember that the Philistines didn't like God and His people. They soon fought another war against the Lord's people and killed King Saul and his son, Jonathan. The Philistines believed they were winning, but they were wrong! God had other plans. He had not said David would be king for nothing. He also had plans for His people, and He was not going to allow the Philistines to win.

And that's the way it happened. The Lord helped David and his men to defeat the Philistines. God also gave David a very special city to live in—Jerusalem. David wanted God always to be there with him and the people. He knew that the Lord is actually everywhere, but the Lord promised to be with them in Jerusalem in a very special way. That's why, later on, a temple for the Lord was built in Jerusalem.

If we believe in God, He will be with us in a special way.

Remember: God loves us in a special way.

David helps others

April 13 2 Samuel 9

David said to Mephibosheth, "I want to be kind to you. I promised Jonathan."
(2 Sam. 9:1)

David never forgot his friend Jonathan. He promised him that he would always help him and his children whenever he could.

The Philistines killed Jonathan, but he had a son who was still alive. The boy, Mephibosheth, fell when he was little and hurt both legs badly so it was difficult for him to walk.

When David became king, he didn't forget his promise. When he heard that Mephibosheth was still alive, he sent someone to get him right away. David was very kind to Mephibosheth. He took care of him as he had promised Jonathan. Jonathan had been dead for a long time, but David kept his promise. If we make a promise, we should keep it.

If we love the Lord, we must never promise to do something and then not do it. A promise is a promise!

Remember: Never, ever lie!

The Lord takes care of David

April 14 Psalm 16

Please keep me safe, Lord. You are my shelter. (Ps. 16:1)

David knew he couldn't do anything without the Lord. He wrote a beautiful poem, Psalm 16. In it, he says how important the Lord is to him. The Lord is with him all the time, which makes him happy and makes him feel safe. He isn't afraid anymore. This is what David wrote:

"Lord, let me be with You always. Keep me safe, God. I am Yours. To me, nothing is more important or better than You. I want to have nothing to do with people who don't love You.

"Lord, You take care of me. Everything I have, You gave me. It is because of You that I am alive. I am so happy with everything You have given me—thank You very much. Thank You, too, for teaching me to do the right thing, because You are always with me. With You, I am safe. You teach me the right way to live. You give me only good things. I'm glad that I can always be with You."

The Lord does all this for every one of His children. If we believe in Him, we are His children. He will take good care of us. We need to remember to thank Him every day!

Remember: Thank the Lord for everything He does for us.

April 15 Psalm 139

Lord, You know me; You made me

Lord, You know everything about me. (Ps. 139:1)

There was once a man who wondered if he could hide from the Lord. Would he be able to do something secretly, so that no one knew—not even the Lord? That man was David. This is what he says in Psalm 139:7-12:

"Is there a place I can go where God is not there? I tried hiding in the graveyard, but God was there. I tried to go as far east as I could, and to the west, but I couldn't hide from God, because He was everywhere.

"Then I tried hiding from God in the darkness. But to God it's never really dark. He can see in the dark. Then I knew that the Lord knows what I think, almost before I have thought it. He knows what I am going to say, and what I am not going to say. When I sit down or stand up, the Lord knows it, because He made me. Even before I was born, He already knew me. Even then He held me close, because He loved me."

The Lord loves us and knows each one of us just as much as He loved and knew David.

Remember: The Lord never stops loving us.

David says thank you to God

April 16 Psalm 23

Your goodness and love will be with me all my life. (Ps. 23:6)

Imagine there's a man who is so poor he doesn't even have food to eat. He has to live on the scraps he can pick up. Suddenly, a rich man comes along and invites him to dinner. He gives him only the best food and most delicious cold drinks and tells the poor man to eat and drink as much as he wants. How would the poor man feel? He would probably be very happy. This is how David feels about God, because God treats him so well. In Psalm 23, David says God is like the rich man who invites someone to a scrumptious dinner. This is what David says:

"Lord, you invite me to a feast. You make me feel so important. You are so kind and nice to me. Now those who made fun of me are silent. They have nothing to say."

David never gets tired of talking about the goodness of the Lord. God looks after all His children like this. We must remember to say thank you.

Remember: God looks after all His children.

Trust the Lord

April 17 Psalm 146

Don't put your trust in people. (Ps. 146:3)

There was once a man called Peter who learned a very important lesson. He trusted a rich and powerful king who promised to help him. Peter had to work for him and serve him. Peter thought, "Now I'm going to be very important, too, and have everything I want." That's what the king promised him. Peter forgot all about God and served only the king. Then the king died, and Peter was left on his own ...

In the Bible there was a man like Peter, and this is what he learned:

"Don't put your trust in powerful or important people. They are, after all, only human beings. They aren't always going to be there to help you. One day they will die, and then they can't do what they promised anymore. It's much better to put your trust in the Lord and to serve Him. He never dies. He will always be there to help you. The happiest person is the one who trusts the Lord."

This should be a lesson to us too.

Remember: We can always trust the Lord.

David makes a mistake

April 18 2 Samuel 24

"Lord, I have made a mistake. Please forgive me." (2 Sam. 24:10)

One day, David decided to go and check how many soldiers he had. If he had plenty, he thought he wouldn't have to rely on the Lord so much. Then he realized this was a mistake. Having a big army was not enough. He should be putting his trust in God alone. God sent a messenger to David. "The Lord gives you three choices," the messenger said. "You must choose one:
- For seven years there will be no food.
- Your enemies will chase you for three months, and you will constantly be on the run.
- The people will be very sick for three days."

David wondered which one he should choose. Finally, he chose the three days of sickness. At the end of the first day, seventy thousand people were dead. When David heard this, he felt terrible. He begged the Lord to punish him instead. So the Lord gave him a second chance. If he would promise to obey Him always, God would forgive him. David promised, and the Lord forgave him.

Remember: If we sin, and then confess, God will forgive us.

The Lord will watch over you

April 19 Psalm 91

With the Lord you are safe. You can trust Him. (Ps. 91:2)

Life can be very difficult. One day someone is fine, and the next day he gets sick. We really want him to get better immediately but he doesn't. David desperately wanted to build the Lord a temple but the Lord wouldn't let him.

In Psalm 91, we learn not to lose heart when things go wrong. God will tell the angels to protect us. If we are scared, we should pray to the Lord. He will hear our prayers, and because He loves us He will keep us safe. Remember that the Lord is very powerful. Nobody is stronger than He is, so we can trust in Him.

The Lord is there to help us and, when we are in trouble, we can rely on Him.

Remember: We shouldn't lose faith if things go wrong.

Without the Lord, the work is useless

April 20 Psalm 127

The Lord takes care of His loved ones. (Ps. 127:2)

David really wanted to build a temple for the Lord, but the Lord didn't want him to do it. The Lord wanted Solomon, David's son, to build Him the temple. Sometimes things don't work out the way we want them to, because the Lord knows better. If the Lord isn't happy with something, we should just accept it.

This is what Solomon, the man who finally built the temple in Jerusalem, says in Psalm 127: "Unless the Lord helps build the house, the work of the builders is useless. If the Lord doesn't protect us, nobody can protect us. Our whole lives are in the hands of the Lord. People who do things with the help of the Lord, rather than trying to do them on their own, do them so much better."

We should always try our best. It doesn't matter if we lose, however hard we tried to win. It's much more important to do our best to use the talents the Lord has given us.

Remember: We should ask the Lord to do things with us.

David is disobedient

April 21 2 Samuel 11

What David had done did not please the Lord. (2 Sam. 11:27)

There was a war going on, and David's soldiers had to go and fight. David stayed at home. One afternoon, he saw a beautiful woman. She was Bathsheba, the wife of one of David's soldiers. David liked her and asked her to come and visit him. He knew it was wrong and meant disobeying the Lord.

A while later, the woman told David she was going to have his baby. David knew he couldn't hide the foolish thing he had done any longer. He tried to think of a way to solve the problem. Eventually, he sent Uriah, Bathsheba's husband, to fight on the front line. David hoped the enemy would kill Uriah, and that's what happened. David was pleased because he could marry Bathsheba before the baby was born, and he thought nobody would notice that he had been disobedient.

But God knew. We can't hide anything from Him. He knows every single thing that happens in our lives.

Remember: God knows everything.

David is punished

April 22 2 Samuel 12

"Why didn't you obey the Lord?" (2 Sam. 12:9)

One day, Nathan, a prophet of God, visited David. He told David this story: There was a poor man whose only friend was a little lamb. He played with it and fed it with food from his own plate. At night, they slept on the same bed. He loved this little lamb very much.

Nearby, lived a rich man who owned many sheep. One day, the rich man had a visitor. The rich man wondered what to serve for dinner that night. Then he saw the poor man's little lamb. "Kill that lamb," he told his servants. So they slaughtered the poor man's lamb.

When David heard this story, he was furious with the rich man. "Any man who does such a thing deserves to die," he cried. "Bring that man to me immediately!" Nathan answered, "You are the man. You had another man killed and took his wife." Then David knew the Lord had seen how disobedient he had been. He was so ashamed, and he felt terrible. He asked the Lord to forgive him.

We can't hide anything from the Lord.

Remember: We can't hide anything from the Lord.

David is sad, because he disappointed the Lord

April 23 Psalm 38

Please do not leave me, Lord. Do not go away. (Ps. 38:21)

David was heartbroken, because he had disappointed God. He had had a man killed so that he could have his wife. During this time, he wrote Psalm 38. This is his prayer:

"Lord, please don't leave me alone. Please stay with me. Don't let go of my hand. I know I have done a terrible thing, Lord. Help me, please Lord.

"I feel like someone who has been shot with an arrow. I hurt so much it feels as if my whole body is covered with big sores. Lord, only You can make it better. Please forgive me. I want to obey You always, and I will. I want to do what You want me to."

God didn't abandon David and, if we make a mistake, He won't leave us either. We shouldn't be ashamed to tell Him we're sorry. He knows all about it anyway. We just need to go to Him and ask Him to forgive us, and He will!

Remember: We don't need to be ashamed to ask the Lord's forgiveness.

Absalom turns against his father

April 24 2 Samuel 15

"None of us will escape from Absalom." (2 Sam. 15:14)

The Lord gives us mothers and fathers to take care of us. He wants us to respect them. King David had a son who didn't obey him, and it made David very sad.

Absalom, David's eldest son, was big and handsome, but his heart was rotten. He didn't care if he hurt others or cheated them—including his own father. As king, his father David had to punish people who did wrong things. Absalom would go to the people and tell them that his father was no good. He said that if he became king he wouldn't punish them. Absalom stirred up the people against David, even though David was his father.

One day, Absalom told David he was going to Hebron to worship the Lord. In fact, he was plotting rebellion against the king. David was taken by surprise. He had to flee from Absalom and his soldiers. Absalom took his father's place in the palace. His father had to go into hiding. But this was not the end of the story.

Remember: We should love and respect our parents.

Absalom dies

April 25 2 Samuel 17-18

"O Absalom, my son, my son! If only I could have died instead of you!" (2 Sam. 18:33)

David's soldiers were angry when Absalom took his father's place in the palace. They went to David and told him they would help him. David's troops didn't want him to be killed, so they went into battle without him. David asked them not to harm his son, Absalom.

It was a bloody battle. David's soldiers fought hard and won. Absalom tried to escape on a mule but, as he rode under a tree, his long hair got caught in the thick branches. The mule ran on, leaving Absalom dangling in the tree. That's where David's soldiers found him and killed him.

David went back to live in the palace again, and he ruled the way God wanted. He was sad about the death of his son. Even though Absalom had treated him so badly, he still loved him.

Remember: Moms and dads love their children.

Our lives are in the Lord's hands

April 26 Psalm 31

I *trust you, Lord.* (Ps. 31:14)

Things don't always work out the way we want them to. Even if we are Christians, bad things can still happen to us. The difference is, the Lord can help us when these things happen. Someone who doesn't love the Lord has no one like Him to help him or her.

David writes in Psalm 31 that things went so terribly wrong for him at times that he thought he was going to die. He often said to himself, "I've had it!" He even thought the Lord had forgotten about him. People were mean and made fun of him. Even his own friends wanted nothing to do with him. David felt very lonely, but he never lost hope because he knew how much the Lord loved him.

David trusted the Lord. He felt safe, because he could rely on the Lord to help him. The Lord looks after His children, so if we are children of the Lord we have nothing to worry about. The Lord will help us.

Remember: The Lord keeps His children close to Him.

Solomon becomes a good king

April 27 1 Kings 3

"Lord, help me so that I can tell the difference between right and wrong." (1 Kings 3:9)

After David's death, his son Solomon became king. Solomon loved the Lord very much, just like his father had.

One day, the Lord said to Solomon in a dream, "What do you want, Solomon? Ask, and I will give it to you."

"Lord," said Solomon, "I am still very young. I don't always know the right thing to do, but I must rule over Your people. Help me so that I will always listen to You. Let me make the right choices. If You don't help me, I can't be a good king."

The Lord was very pleased with Solomon's answer. Solomon could have asked for anything—to be rich or successful or to live for a long time. But he didn't think of himself. He asked God to give him wisdom so he would rule the people with justice and fairness. The Lord made Solomon wiser than anybody before or after him, and he was a very good king.

It's always worth listening to the Lord and serving Him. Solomon knew that.

Remember: It's a pleasure to serve the Lord.

Solomon builds a temple

April 28 1 Kings 6 & 8

"The Lord is wonderful. He has kept the promise He made to my father, David." (1 Kings 8:15)

Solomon was a good king who listened to the Lord and did what He said. Solomon wanted to build a temple for the Lord. God said to him, "I want you to build Me a temple. Then I will be able to stay with you and My people in a special way. But it's not just the temple that's important. I also want My people to serve Me with all their hearts."

Solomon built a temple. It was beautiful inside. He brought the ark to the temple, and it was a sign that God was there.

The people were very happy, and they celebrated because the Lord was there with them. The Ten Commandments that God gave Moses on Mount Sinai were in the ark. From that time on, God was in the temple among His people in a very special way.

But God is not only in a building. He also lives inside us. Whatever we are doing, He is with us.

Remember: God is with always with us.

Solomon is clever

April 29 1 Kings 3-4

God Himself gave Solomon wisdom. (1 Kings 3:28)

The Lord made Solomon very wise.

One day, two women came to Solomon. They lived in the same house. Their babies were born at about the same time. One baby died when its mother rolled over on it by accident one night. She got up and quietly switched the two babies. She put the dead one down next to the other woman. The next morning when the woman woke up, she saw immediately that the dead baby was not hers. The two women started arguing. Both said the other one was lying. Solomon had to help them solve the problem.

Solomon listened carefully. Then he said, "Bring the live baby here, and bring me a sword. Cut the child in two, and give each woman half!"

The real mother was heartbroken. She couldn't bear her baby to be killed. She cried out, "Oh no, give her the child. Please don't kill him." Then Solomon knew she was the real mother. He said, "You are the mother." The news spread, and the people who heard about it knew that God had made Solomon very wise.

Remember: God created us.

The Lord takes good care of His people

April 30 1 Kings 10:1-13

"It is because the Lord loves His people that He gave them such a good king." (1 Kings 10:9)

Solomon was a very wise man. People all over the world heard how intelligent he was. A beautiful queen, the Queen of Sheba, lived in a faraway land. She also heard about Solomon. People said he was rich and that the Lord took care of him. She decided to go and visit King Solomon. She wanted to see for herself if he really was that clever and rich, so she packed many gifts of gold and diamonds and set off to visit Solomon.

She asked Solomon the most difficult questions she could think of. She was amazed as she listened to him answer every one. She realized why Solomon was so wise. The Lord loved him and was good to him. The Lord loved His people too, and He wanted their king, Solomon, to be a good ruler. When the queen went back home, she knew that the Lord takes good care of His people.

Remember: God looks after His children.

May 1 Proverbs 2-3

Good advice for children

Discuss everything you do with the Lord. Then He will show you the right way. (Prov. 3:6)

Solomon loved children. He wanted them to grow up the right way so he gave them some very good advice. He said:
- Always listen to good advice. Good advice is advice that tells us what the Lord wants us to do.
- Be honest, and never lie or cheat.
- Never even think about doing something that's wrong.
- Always love others.
- People must be able to trust us. When they talk about us, they should be able to say, "They never lie. So you can always believe them."
- Pray often. Ask the Lord to help you do the right thing every day.
- Go to church, and show you love the Lord.
- If you do something wrong, remember that the Lord can discipline you, like a father disciplines his child. This doesn't mean that He doesn't love you. He does love you, but He wants to teach you the difference between right and wrong.

Remember: Do what pleases God.

More good advice for children

May 2 Proverbs 3

The person who understands what the Lord expects from him or her will be happy. (Prov. 3:13)

If we live the way the Lord wants us to, we will enjoy life. Remember that the Lord made us. He knows what will make us happy and what will not.
- Be kind, and help people when you can.
- Never hurt someone's feelings by being rude or by shouting at them.
- Don't worry too much or get scared. Remember that the Lord loves us. He will protect us.
- Never gossip or say or think nasty things about people. People who do this will be punished.
- If you're stronger than your friends, don't hurt or bully them. The Lord doesn't like that at all.
- Never think you're better than others or make fun of anybody.
- Don't be rude and make others feel uncomfortable.

Remember: Be kind to other people.

Don't be lazy

May 3 Proverbs 6

Take a lesson from the ants, you lazybones. See how they work, and learn from them! (Prov. 6:6)

Solomon knew what the Lord expects from people. The Lord sees every step we take. If we do something wrong, the Lord sees it and will punish us. His advice was:

Don't be lazy. Watch the ants and see how hard they work. They don't have teachers or leaders. They have no one to tell them what to do, but when winter comes and it's difficult to find food, they have stored up more than enough. They worked all summer to do this. Let this be a lesson to us. It's good to do our duty and to work hard. Lazy people get nothing done. They say, "I want to sleep a little later. I just want to rest a little longer." They lie around all day, doing nothing. Such people shouldn't think they are going to get something for nothing. They are going to struggle for their whole lives.

The Lord likes hard-working children. He gives us many gifts—strength and good health and talents. He doesn't want us to waste these. That is why He is pleased when we use our strength and our talents.

Remember: The Lord likes diligent children.

Don't cheat others

May 4 Proverbs 6

My child, listen to what your father and mother tell you. Keep it in your heart. (Prov. 6:20-21)

Solomon had more good advice. Someone who lies to others is no good, he said. They make trouble wherever they go. The Lord doesn't like people who are always lying and fighting.

Children should listen when their fathers and mothers speak. They will try to give their children the best advice. We know they don't want their children to hurt others or do wrong things. Imagine that someone's in a pitch-dark room. He can't see anything and doesn't know what to do. The good advice of a mom and dad is like a light shining into that dark room. Suddenly, he knows what to do and what not to do. If we listen to the good advice of our parents, we will be happy.

The Lord gave our parents the responsibility to teach us what is right and what is wrong. We need to listen to them. Read the Bible with them every day, and pray with them.

Remember: We must obey our parents.

More good advice

May 5 Proverbs 7-10

A *cheerful heart is good medicine.* (Prov. 17:22)

Solomon goes on to say in Proverbs:
- Having a good friend is better than being rich and having no friends.
- Stay away from anyone who is out to hurt you. If you get too close to such a person, he will burn you like fire.
- A wise person thinks first and then speaks. It is stupid to speak without thinking.
- People with a friendly smile make everyone around them happy.
- We can plan what we want to do, but it is God who decides if it will really happen.
- Don't tell stories about others, even if everybody likes listening.
- People who know the Lord don't get angry unless they have a good reason.
- It is better to be honest and to stay poor than to cheat people and get rich.
- Don't fight back if someone fights with you. Then the person will stop, because it's no fun anymore.

Remember: Be friendly and make others happy.

Enjoy life while you are young

May 6 Ecclesiastes 11-12

It's wonderful to be young. Enjoy every minute of it. Do everything you want to do, but remember: you will have to explain everything you do to the Lord. (Eccl. 11:9)

Solomon had special advice for young people.

They should be happy to be alive, remembering that they won't live forever. Just as the night draws near, so death comes closer. It shouldn't frighten us. Instead, we should enjoy life every day.

Solomon goes on to say that young people should enjoy life while they can because, before they know it, they'll be old. Their chance to be young will be over. They should do everything they enjoy doing, but they should make sure that it's not something that will displease the Lord. They shouldn't do anything that makes them feel bad or that is going to hurt themselves or others. Young people should do what is right and remember to love the Lord. Then if things go wrong, they will have someone to help them.

Remember: Enjoy life.

Live every day to the full

May 7 Ecclesiastes 5 & 9

It is good for people to enjoy the life the Lord has given them. (Eccl. 5:18)

Solomon said that, even if things go wrong, we must still enjoy life.

Often things happen to us that we don't like. We get upset and unhappy. But remember, it will pass.

If things aren't going the way we would like, we should try thinking about all the good things the Lord gives us. We have food, clothes, and a place to sleep. We can get up tomorrow morning and live for the Lord. These are all presents the Lord gives us, and they should make us very happy. Solomon asks who can eat or be happy if the Lord doesn't make it all happen.

Where do all the good things we have come from? The Lord gives us everything. Surely He wants us to enjoy what He gives us.

Remember: The Lord wants us to enjoy what He has given us.

A time for everything

May 8 Ecclesiastes 2-3

Be happy, and enjoy everything the Lord gives you. (Eccl. 3:13)

Life is not always the same. It changes. Sometimes we are sad. Sometimes we are glad. Sometimes a person plants a tree, and sometimes he chops it down. Sometimes we like someone and sometimes not. There is a time for everything.

The Lord wants us to enjoy life—when things go well and also when they don't. He wants to be proud of us. We shouldn't be careless when we do something, because we are special to the Lord. He has put us in a very special place in life.

We don't always understand why some things happen, but we believe that the Lord knows best. We shouldn't give up hope. Even when we're having a hard time, we should thank the Lord for all the good things He gives us.

If things happen in our lives that make us unhappy, we shouldn't sit around and mope but think about all our blessings.

Remember: Each one of us is unique in the eyes of the Lord.

Don't listen to the advice of wicked friends

May 9 1 Kings 12

The people asked the king to treat them well. (1 Kings 12:4)

After King Solomon's death, his son Rehoboam became king. He was still young and didn't know how to rule the people. Should he be strict, or should he be friendly? If he was strict with them, they might get angry. If he was friendly with them, they might not do what he told them. He decided to ask the older people what to do. They told him to be friendly. Rehoboam still wasn't sure that this was good advice, so he asked his friends who were the same age as he was. They said he should be strict. They said if people didn't listen to him he should punish them. Rehoboam took the bad advice of his friends, and the people became angry with him. They rebelled.

We have to be careful whose advice we take, even if it is our friends' advice. We should think carefully whether it's good or bad advice and only take it if it's good advice.

Remember: Don't listen to bad advice.

The king starts worshiping idols

May 10 1 Kings 12-13

"Please ask the Lord to help me." (1 Kings 13:6)

King Jeroboam reigned in the country, not in a city. He was worried that people would prefer the city of Jerusalem, because there was a beautiful temple there, so he built his own temple. But he didn't build it to serve the Lord. He put two golden calves in the temple. Jeroboam told the people to worship these calf idols and even appointed priests for these gods.

One day, Jeroboam was worshiping the gods. He brought a sacrifice to offer on the altar. A man of God, a prophet, came to him and said, "All these evil priests are going to be killed. I will give you a sign to show you that I am telling the truth. This altar will split apart." King Jeroboam pointed his finger at the prophet and told the guards, "Grab that man!" As soon as he spoke, the king's hand became paralyzed in that position.

Jeroboam begged the prophet to make his hand work again, so the man prayed to God. The king regained the use of his hand. He learned his lesson—never to worship idols but to serve only the true God.

Remember: We shouldn't serve anybody except the Lord.

We must obey the Lord

May 11 1 Kings 13

"You have disobeyed the Lord!" (1 Kings 13:21-22)

If the Lord asks us to do something, we must do what He says. There was once a prophet who took an important message to the king. The king wanted to treat him to a nice meal, but the prophet answered that the Lord had told him not to eat anything before he was back home.

On his way home, he met someone who lied and said an angel had come to him and told him to give the prophet food to eat and water to drink. The two of them went to the man's house. While they were eating, God sent the prophet a message: "You did not do what the Lord told you, so you won't be buried in your hometown." As the prophet made his way home after the meal, a lion attacked him and killed him. The man who had lied to him heard the news. He went to get the prophet's body and buried it. "This is what happens if you don't do as you're told," he said.

Even if our best friend says to do something that we know is not what the Lord wants, we shouldn't listen.

Remember: God's children do what God wants them to do.

Elijah and the ravens

May 12 1 Kings 17

The Lord sent ravens to bring Elijah food. (1 Kings 17:4)

King Ahab ruled over God's people. He was married to Jezebel. She was not one of God's people. She didn't like the Lord, and she worshiped another god. His name was Baal. She wanted Israel to worship Baal instead of God, and she built lots of temples for this false god.

God was angry. He wanted to show the people He was the strongest and that Baal was useless. He did something that only God can do. He sent His prophet, Elijah, to Ahab. Elijah told the king, "From now on, there will not be a drop of rain. The Lord will decide when the rain will fall again." From that day on, there was no rain.

The king was angry with Elijah for bringing such bad news. Elijah had to go into hiding. He camped beside a brook in the fields. Nobody knew where he was, but the Lord looked after him. God sent the ravens to take Elijah food to eat every day.

Remember: Only worship God. He takes care of us.

May 13 1 Kings 17

A widow takes care of Elijah

"The Lord says there will always be plenty of flour in the jar." (1 Kings 17:14)

For a long time, there was not a drop of rain. The plants died. The rivers dried up.

Elijah was very hungry and thirsty. A woman lived near where he was hiding. Her husband had died, and she was very poor. Elijah went to her and asked for some water. She didn't mind helping Elijah. He also asked her for a bite of bread. The woman wanted to give Elijah some bread, but she only had a handful of flour and a little cooking oil left. When that was gone there would be nothing left for her and her son to eat. But then a wonderful thing happened. Elijah told the woman to make some food for the three of them. Even though there was not nearly enough flour, God would help her. The woman did what Elijah said. She trusted the Lord and started baking bread and, to her surprise, no matter how much oil and flour she used, there was always enough left in the jars. It was a miracle. Only God can do something like that!

Even if we sometimes have a hard time, we shouldn't lose heart. God knows best, and He will help us.

Remember: The Lord can do wonderful things.

The Lord can help us

May 14 1 Kings 17

"Now I know for sure you are a man of God. What you say is true. The Lord speaks through you!" (1 Kings 17:24)

Elijah stayed with the widow and her little boy. It was better than staying in the field by the brook. The widow helped him and cooked for him. One day, her son got sick. He grew worse and worse, and finally he died. The widow was very sad. She asked Elijah if God was angry with her. What had she done wrong? Why did her little boy die?

Elijah comforted her and told her she could trust the Lord. He said she should bring the boy to his room. He put the boy down on his bed, then kneeled down and prayed. "Lord, please don't let a terrible thing like this happen to this woman. She helped me. Please let this child come back to life."

After Elijah had prayed, the Lord brought the child back to life. Elijah took him to his mother. She was so happy, and she knew it was God who had helped her.

When we feel sad, we should pray and ask the Lord to help us—and He will, in His own way.

Remember: We should always pray when we are feeling sad.

Elijah proves there is only one true God

May 15 1 Kings 18

"O Lord, answer me so these people will know that You are God." (1 Kings 18:37)

Many people thought Baal, an idol, was stronger than the Lord. Queen Jezebel told them it was so. But Elijah knew that only the Lord was really God. One day, the Lord told Elijah to show the people how powerful He is.

Elijah challenged all the priests of Baal: "Let Baal come and light a fire for us all to see." The priests of Baal brought wood for the fire and put it on the altar. They prayed and prayed all day long, but nothing happened. They kept on praying even when they were exhausted, but still nothing happened. Elijah mocked them: "Shout louder," he said. "Maybe your god is asleep!" Then Elijah took 12 stones and made an altar. He piled wood on the altar and put the offering on top. "Now bring water, and pour it on the wood," Elijah said. This was to make sure Elijah couldn't trick them and somehow light the fire. Then he asked the Lord to light the fire. Immediately, before their very eyes, the Lord flashed down fire from heaven. Then the people knew: God is the only God, and He is much more powerful than Baal is. Then and there, they killed the priests of Baal.

Our Lord is real, and He is very powerful.

Remember: The Lord really exists!

God sends rain

May 16 1 Kings 18

The Lord gave special strength to Elijah. (1 Kings 18:46)

The Lord was very angry when the people started believing in the god Baal, and He told them that He was the only true God. But there were people who didn't believe Him. So God showed again how powerful He is. He said it would not rain again until He said so. The drought was terrible, and Elijah decided to ask the Lord to please send rain again.

Elijah climbed to the top of a high mountain and prayed. At first, nothing happened. But Elijah didn't stop praying.

When Elijah was praying for the seventh time, his friend told him he could see a little cloud on the horizon. It was only the size of a man's hand. Elijah knew immediately that the Lord had answered his prayer. He ran to tell the king, but it started raining hard before he reached the palace.

We really can trust the Lord. If we pray, and He doesn't answer us the first time, we can ask again. He will answer us, in His own time.

Remember: Pray often. It's the only way to speak to God.

May 17 1 Kings 19

The queen wants to kill Elijah

"Lord, I have served you heart and soul." (1 Kings 19:14)

Jezebel was a wicked queen. She wanted the Israelites to worship her gods. Elijah had proved that Baal was useless, which made Jezebel very angry. She decided to kill Elijah, and he had to hide in the desert. He was frightened and miserable. It seemed to him that Jezebel had killed everyone who loved God and that he was the only one left. He worked so hard for God, and yet he had to hide. He couldn't understand why. Suddenly, an angel stood before him. The angel gave him food and water and told him to eat so that he could regain his strength. The Lord still had a lot of work for him to do.

Elijah walked to Mount Horeb and waited for the Lord. First, a mighty windstorm hit the mountain, and afterwards there was a terrible earthquake. After the earthquake, there was a fire. But the Lord was not in any of these. Then the Lord came past, very quietly. God comforted Elijah and reminded him that He always protects His children. We need to remember that, too. We don't need to worry, because the Lord will protect us.

Remember: The Lord will always be with us.

God gives His people another messenger

May 18 2 Kings 1-2

"Where is the Lord, the God of Elijah?" (2 Kings 2:14)

Elijah served the Lord faithfully, but he was coming to the end of his life. He had a very good friend called Elisha. The two of them went to the Jordan River. Elijah took his cloak and struck the water with it. Suddenly, the river opened up, and there was a path that led to the other side. When they reached the other side, Elijah asked Elisha, "What can I do for you before I die?" Elisha answered, "I want to be just like you." Suddenly, they saw a chariot of fire drawn by horses of fire. It stopped between Elisha and Elijah. Then a whirlwind carried Elijah into heaven.

When Elijah disappeared, his cloak was left behind. Elisha picked it up and struck the water with it. Then he asked God to help him. Suddenly a path opened up across the river, and everybody realized that Elisha was like Elijah—a man of God. The people of Jericho asked him to help them. The water in their town was so foul that they couldn't drink it. He asked for a bowl of salt and put the salt in the water. Immediately, the water became pure and drinkable.

Remember: The Lord gives us leaders to help us.

The Lord helps in wonderful ways

May 19 2 Kings 4

"You know my husband served the Lord." (2 Kings 4:1)

One day, a woman who was very poor came to Elisha the prophet. Her husband, who had served the Lord faithfully, had died. She had no one to provide for her anymore, and she had no money to buy food. She'd borrowed money from other people but couldn't pay them back. They wanted their money and threatened to put her in jail.

The woman begged Elisha to help her. Elisha asked her what she had. "Nothing at all, except a little bit of cooking oil," she said. Elisha told her to borrow as many empty bottles as she could from her friends and to fill them with cooking oil from her bottle. She did as he said.

Amazingly, she poured and poured but the oil didn't run out until all the bottles were full. The woman was able to sell the oil and pay her debts. She even had enough money left over to live on.

The Lord takes care of people who need Him in amazing ways.

Remember: God helps those who need Him.

An ax floats on the water

May 20 2 Kings 2 & 6

And the ax floated on the water. (2 Kings 6:6)

Elisha did many wonderful things, because the Lord helped him. One day, he went with some men who wanted to build a place to live. As one of the men was chopping down a tree, his ax fell into the river. The man was worried. The ax didn't belong to him. He had borrowed it. He didn't know what to do. Elisha asked, "Where did it fall in?" The man showed him, and Elisha cut a stick and threw it into the water where the ax had fallen. The ax floated up to the surface of the water. The man stretched out his hand and grabbed it. Sometimes, the Lord makes things happen that we don't expect.

Another day, Elisha was on his way to worship. Some boys made fun of him because he was bald. "Go away, you baldy!" they teased him. Elisha turned around. He warned them to stop. He was God's servant. When they made fun of him, they were mocking God. The boys wouldn't listen. Then two bears came out of the woods and attacked the boys. Forty-two boys died.

We need to show respect for the Lord. If we do, we will make Him happy.

Remember: We should always show respect for the Lord.

Will the Lord help?

May 21 2 Kings 6

"If the Lord doesn't help you, what can I do?" (2 Kings 6:27)

The king of Aram and his whole army went to Samaria. The king wanted to take the city and ordered his soldiers to surround it. Nobody could enter or leave the city. The people couldn't go out to get food or water. Eventually, they ate all the available food. They started getting very hungry, but there was nothing to eat. Even a donkey's head cost a lot of money. They were so hungry they paid a lot of money to have dove droppings to eat!

A woman asked the king to help her. She told him how hungry they were. She and her friend had decided to eat their children—one day her son and the next day her friend's son. They ate her son first, but when it was the other woman's turn, she hid her son.

When the king heard this, he was shocked. He said to the woman, "I can't help you. Only the Lord can. Only He can save us from the terrible situation we're in."

Then he went to Elisha the prophet and said, "I don't think the Lord can help us anymore."

Remember: We know the Lord can help us.

Nothing is impossible for the Lord

May 22 2 Kings 7

This is what the Lord says, "By this time tomorrow you will have more than enough food." (2 Kings 7:1)

The Lord helps His people, and Elisha was able to tell the king, "The Lord has good news for you. Food is very scarce now. But, by this time tomorrow, you will be able to buy a big bag of flour for next to nothing."

"Impossible!" many people said.

Then four men in the city decided to join the enemy. If they stayed in the city they would die of hunger, so if they left and the enemy killed them it wouldn't matter anyway. But there was a chance that they might not be killed and be given something to eat. When they reached the enemy camp, there was no one there! The Lord had sent a noise that sounded like a great army approaching, and when the enemy soldiers heard it, they panicked and ran off leaving all their food and money behind. The four men went back to the city and told the guards. The gates were flung open, and the people ran out of the city and helped themselves to food.

Elisha's words came true. Nothing is impossible for the Lord.

Remember: Anything is possible for the Lord.

Our Lord is everywhere and always there for us

May 23 1 Kings 20

"Then you will know that I am the Lord." (1 Kings 20:28)

The people who didn't like the Lord wanted to take Israel's country. They thought the Israelites worshiped mountain gods, so they would be able to defeat them easily if they fought them on the plains, since their gods wouldn't be there. They assembled a great army to fight against Israel. The Israelite army looked like a little flock of goats in comparison, but the Israelites weren't afraid.

The battle started. Even though there were very few Israelites, they had the Lord to help them. A hundred thousand of the enemy died. The rest ran away to hide behind the walls of a nearby city. But the city wall fell in on them, killing twenty-seven thousand men.

The enemies of Israel learned their lesson that day. They discovered that the God of the Israelites was everywhere and always ready to help His people.

Remember: The Lord is always with us.

Don't be disobedient

May 24 1 Kings 20

"Well, it's your own fault. You have decided on your own punishment." (1 Kings 20:40)

The king of Aram, who thought the Lord lived only on mountains, soon found out how wrong he was. So he told Ahab, the king of the Israelites, how sorry he was about everything. He wanted to be King Ahab's friend, and Ahab was flattered. He believed what the king of Aram said. But the Lord was not happy. He told one of His prophets, "Get someone to beat you up so you're black-and-blue." The prophet obeyed and afterwards bandaged up his face. He stood by the side of the road, and King Ahab didn't even recognize him when he passed by.

Then the prophet said, "Sir, I had to guard a prisoner. I was told, 'If he gets away you will either die or pay a fine.' While I was busy doing something else, the prisoner escaped."

"Well," King Ahab said, "you have brought your punishment on yourself."

Then the prophet took the bandage off. "Sir, you have just brought punishment on yourself. The Lord told you to kill that king. Now you will have to die in his place." We should always do what the Lord tells us to do.

Remember: We need to obey the Lord.

May 25 2 Kings 15

The Lord shows His power

"I know, at last, there is no God in all the world except the God of Israel." (2 Kings 5:15)

A certain man called Naaman became very sick. Nobody could make him well again. Naaman didn't know God. But there was a young girl who did know God, and she knew He could help people. She worked for Naaman's wife, and she told Naaman to go and see a prophet who would help him. First, Naaman went to the king of Israel and asked for his help. The king was sad. He couldn't heal people.

When Elisha the prophet heard about it, he suggested that Naaman come to see him. Naaman stopped at Elisha's house. Elisha didn't even come to the door. He sent Naaman a message: "Go and wash yourself seven times in the Jordan River."

Naaman was furious. He thought Elisha would do something special, or at least see him. He decided to go home. But his friends said he might as well follow Elisha's advice. After all, it wasn't difficult. Naaman did what Elisha had told him, and the Lord healed him. He went back to Elisha and said, "Now I know there is no God in all the world except the God of Israel."

Remember: Our God is the only true God.

Honesty is the best policy

May 26 2 Kings 5

"I work for the Lord. I won't take gifts for it." (2 Kings 5:16)

Naaman wanted to give Elisha lots of presents and money, but Elisha wouldn't take anything. Elisha said that the Lord healed Naaman—he didn't do it himself.

Naaman said he wasn't going to worship idols anymore. He now knew who the real God was. He only wanted to serve Him. Then he went on his way home.

Elisha's servant Gehazi overheard their conversation. He thought this was his chance to get his hands on some money, so he ran after Naaman and told him Elisha had sent him because he had changed his mind. He wanted a lot of money and clothes to give two of his friends.

Naaman gave Gehazi much more than he asked for. Gehazi hid it all in his room. But you can't cheat the Lord. When Elisha saw him, he asked, "Where have you been, Gehazi?"

"I haven't been anywhere," he answered. But Elisha knew the truth, and because Gehazi had lied, he got sick with the same disease that Naaman had suffered from. It doesn't pay to lie.

Remember: Dishonesty doesn't pay.

Disobedience is punished

May 27 1 Kings 21

"Ahab, you did not do what the Lord said. You are going to be punished." (1 Kings 21:22)

A man called Naboth had a lovely vineyard. King Ahab wanted this vineyard with its delicious grapes, but Naboth refused to sell it.

Ahab was upset. When he told his wife Jezebel about it, she said, "You're the king. You can do what you want."

Jezebel was an evil queen. She came up with a wicked plan. She arranged a special festival and invited many people. She gave Naboth a seat right at the front and put two crooks next to him. The festival had barely started when these two bad men leaped to their feet. "Naboth has cursed God and the king," they shouted. They took Naboth outside the city walls and stoned him to death. Then Ahab took his vineyard.

But the Lord saw it all. He sent Elijah the prophet to Ahab to tell him that God would punish him and his wife, Jezebel. Elijah's words came true. It's useless to plan evil deeds and think God won't know. He knows everything.

Remember: The Lord sees everything.

Hezekiah was a good king

May 28 2 Kings 20

"O Lord, I have always tried to be faithful to you and to please you." (2 Kings 20:3)

Hezekiah was a good king. He did what the Lord wanted. One day, he became very sick. One of God's prophets visited him and told him that he was going to die. Hezekiah was very sad. He wanted to live a little while longer. He prayed earnestly to the Lord whom he had obeyed all his life.

The prophet was still making his way out of the palace when God sent him back. He had to tell Hezekiah that the Lord had heard his prayer. He would get well and live for another 15 years. Then the prophet told Hezekiah's servants to make an ointment from figs and put it on Hezekiah's sore. They did what he told them to do, and Hezekiah started feeling better right away! Just to make sure that the prophet wasn't lying to him, Hezekiah asked God to give him a sign to prove that he was healed. The Lord said he would make the sun move backwards. It happened, and Hezekiah knew that the Lord had answered his prayer.

Remember: The Lord hears our prayers.

Never forget about the Lord

May 29 2 Kings 20

"This message you have given me from the Lord is good." (2 Kings 20:19)

The news that the Lord had healed Hezekiah spread quickly and as far afield as Babylon.

The Babylonians were planning to take Hezekiah's country from him. They sent people to find out how strong Hezekiah's God was. They had heard about Him, but they wanted to see for themselves.

The spies from Babylon brought many gifts. They made Hezekiah feel so important that he forgot all about the Lord. He showed them everything he owned, even his money and weapons. The spies knew exactly how strong Hezekiah was, but Hezekiah didn't tell them how strong the Lord really was, because he had forgotten about Him.

The spies went back to their king and told him he could defeat Hezekiah. Hezekiah was not really very strong, and they hadn't seen anything of his God. Then God's prophet went to Hezekiah, who had heard what had happened and that the Babylonians were going to attack. But the Lord waited until Hezekiah had died before Israel was taken, so he had peace in his final years.

Remember: Never forget the Lord.

If we don't serve the Lord, it hurts Him

May 30 Hosea 14

"Come back to the Lord." (Hos. 14:2)

The Lord's people, Israel, did not serve Him anymore. They ran after all kinds of gods. The Lord warned them about their behavior. He wanted them to see that what they were doing was wrong.

He sent His prophet Hosea to get married to a very bad woman. Hosea was kind to her, but she was mean to him. Although she was married to Hosea, she had other boyfriends. Hosea was very upset, and the people saw how sad he was. They knew he treated his wife well, even though she treated him like dirt.

Hosea started preaching to the people. He told them that they made the Lord just as sad as he was.

The Lord treated the people well, but they disobeyed Him and ran after heathen gods. They were just like his wife.

They must come back to the Lord, Hosea said. They must stop sinning and promise to serve the Lord again. Then the Lord would take care of them.

Remember: We should not sin but serve the Lord.

May 31 Jeremiah 18

Like clay in the potter's hands

As the clay is in the potter's hand, so are you in My hand. (Jer. 18:6)

God sent Jeremiah, His prophet, to a man who made clay pots and jars. He found the potter working at his wheel. The jar he was making didn't turn out the way he wanted it, so the potter squashed the jar into a lump of clay again.

Patiently, he started all over again, and this time he made a beautiful pot, just as he had planned.

Then the Lord said to Jeremiah, "I am like the potter, and the people are like clay. I can do with them what I like. If they obey Me, I can shape them into lovely jars. If they don't do what I say, I can squash them like clay.

"Tell the people to obey Me. If they live as if I am not here, I will punish them. Then they will be like useless lumps of clay."

But the people wouldn't listen to Jeremiah. They wanted to get rid of him so he wouldn't keep annoying them.

What will God do to these people? They should remember that if they turn against God, He might turn against them.

Remember: The Lord will punish those who don't serve Him.

The people refuse to listen

June 1 Jeremiah 36 & 38

The Lord said, "I will hand over the disobedient people to the king of Babylon." (Jer. 38:3)

The people of Israel were very disobedient. Although the Lord was good to them, they refused to obey Him. Right after worshiping the Lord, they would go and worship other gods. Jeremiah preached and preached. He told them the Lord didn't like them worshiping other gods, but they wouldn't listen.

Finally Jeremiah wrote everything down in a book. The king read the book and then threw it into the fire. The people grabbed Jeremiah and threw him into a water tank that had a thick layer of mud at the bottom. When the king heard about this, he told them to pull Jeremiah out. He talked to Jeremiah secretly and asked him what was wrong. Jeremiah told him God didn't want His people to worship idols. The king wasn't really listening to Jeremiah. He wanted to have his own way, but the Lord would make him pay for his disobedience.

Remember: The Lord will make sinners pay.

The fall of Jerusalem

June 2 Jeremiah 39

The Babylonians burned Jerusalem and the palace and tore down the walls of the city. (Jer. 39:8)

The people of Jerusalem didn't do what the Lord told them. Jeremiah did his best to warn them. He preached all the time, but no one listened to him. They kept on disobeying God and worshiping idols.

The Lord allowed Nebuchadnezzar, the king of Babylon, to attack Jerusalem. Nebuchadnezzar's army was very strong. His soldiers surrounded the city and built a high wall around Jerusalem so that nobody could enter or leave. After four months, the people in the city were starving. They were so hungry that they made a big hole in the wall around the city. The king and his soldiers tried to escape through the hole, but the Babylonians caught them. Then Nebuchadnezzar's soldiers went into the city and tore everything down. Nothing was left standing, not even the beautiful temple. They burned down all the houses and took all the important people to Babylon to work as slaves. They gave their farms away to strangers. The people had thought they could get along without God. They had made a big mistake!

Remember: We can't get along without the Lord.

The exile begins

June 3 2 Kings 25

So the people of Judah were taken from their land. (2 Kings 25:21)

Zedekiah, the king of Jerusalem, tried to escape through a hole in the city's wall. But Nebuchadnezzar's soldiers chased after him and caught him. They took him to Nebuchadnezzar. He was very cruel. First he made Zedekiah watch as they killed his sons in front of him. They blinded Zedekiah, put him in chains, and locked him away in a Babylonian prison.

There, in the foreign land of Babylon, the people began longing for the Lord again. They started feeling sorry that they had not obeyed the Lord. They wished they could worship the Lord again in their own country and in the temple, but they were afraid it was too late.

We shouldn't make the same mistake. We should serve the Lord while we have the chance.

Remember: We must serve the Lord the best we can.

June 4 Daniel 2

The Lord helps where no one else can

Truly your God is the most powerful of all gods. He is more important than kings. He knows everything. (Dan. 2:47)

Daniel was one of the Jews who was captured and taken to Babylon. He was very smart, so the king let him work in the palace.

One night, the king had a dream that scared him. He wanted to know what it meant, so he called all the smartest people together. In case they tried to lie to him, he gave them a test. They had to describe his dream. Of course no one could. How were they supposed to know what he had dreamed?

The king was furious, but then Daniel said he would help him. Daniel prayed to God and asked Him to explain the dream to him. God answered Daniel's prayer, and he went back to the king and was able to tell him exactly what his dream meant. In his dream, the king had seen a huge and powerful statue of a man. The head was made of gold, but the feet were made of clay. The whole statue collapsed and was smashed to bits. Daniel said it meant that Nebuchadnezzar's kingdom would break up like the statue.

King Nebuchadnezzar realized that the Lord had helped Daniel. He said, "Your God is the God of all gods."

Just think, this God is also our God.

Remember: Our God is the God of all gods.

The Lord rescues His children from a fire

June 5 Daniel 3

Our God whom we serve will save us. (Dan. 3:17)

The king of Babylon soon forgot how powerful the Lord is. He made a gold statue and said that everybody had to worship it. Anyone who didn't would be thrown into a blazing fire. Daniel's three friends, Shadrach, Meshach and Abednego, refused. They said they worshiped only the Lord. They knew that, even if they were thrown into the fire, it would be all right, because they trusted the Lord, and He would help them. The king was very angry. He had the fire made seven times hotter and ordered his men to throw Shadrach, Meshach, and Abednego into the flames. The fire was so hot that the men who threw the three friends into the furnace were burned to death. Then an amazing thing happened. In the flames, King Nebuchadnezzar saw, not three, but four men. An angel was there with the three friends.

The king called to them to come out, and Daniel's friends walked out of the fire. Not a hair on their heads was scorched, nor were their clothes burned. They didn't even smell of smoke! Nebuchadnezzar said, "These men really trusted God. They didn't mind dying. It was more important to them to serve the Lord."

Remember: Trust only the Lord.

Daniel thrown to the lions

June 6 Daniel 6

May your God, whom you worship so faithfully, rescue you. (Dan. 6:16)

The king was very fond of Daniel, which made his other officials jealous. They thought of a scheme that would get Daniel into trouble. They knew how much Daniel loved God and that he wouldn't worship anyone else. So they said to the king, "Your Majesty, you are so important and so powerful. Why not make a law that the people must pray only to you for a month?" The king thought this was a good idea, so he made the law. "Anyone who doesn't obey this law will be thrown to the lions," he said. Daniel took no notice of the new law and continued to pray only to the Lord. That was just what his enemies were waiting for. They told the king that Daniel was breaking the law. The king was very sad, but he was forced to throw Daniel to the lions. "I hope your God can help you," he told Daniel.

That night, the king couldn't sleep. Early the next morning, he hurried to the lions' den. He called out to Daniel and was overjoyed when he heard Daniel's voice: "My God sent an angel to shut the lions' mouths."

Daniel was taken out of the lions' den, and his enemies were thrown to the lions and were killed.

Remember: The Lord will deal with bad people.

Don't ever forget about the Lord

June 7 Daniel 4

Everything the Lord does is right. (Dan. 4:37)

Nebuchadnezzar had another dream. He saw a big tree in the middle of the world. It was very tall and strong and reached up to heaven. It had fresh green leaves and was loaded with fruit—enough for all the people in the world. Wild animals rested in its shade, and birds built their nests in its branches. Suddenly, an angel came down from heaven and chopped the tree down. The fruit was thrown away, and the leaves shaken from the branches.

Once again, Nebuchadnezzar called on Daniel to explain this dream. At first, Daniel was too afraid to tell him, but the king insisted. Daniel said, "This tree is actually like you, your Majesty. You have become very great and powerful. Everybody has seen how mighty you are. You think you can do everything, but you have forgotten about the Lord. Just remember, the Lord has not forgotten about you. He will show you who is the mightiest. He will deal with you like the angel dealt with the tree." A year later, Nebuchadnezzar was no longer king. He was like the tree that had been cut down.

Remember: We always need God.

Pride comes before a fall

June 8 Daniel 5

The king started thinking he was better than God. (Dan. 5:20)

Nebuchadnezzar knew exactly how strong the Lord was, but he still forgot about Him. He stopped noticing that the Lord took care of him. Nebuchadnezzar only thought about himself and, because he was so mean to people, everybody was afraid of him. He would kill anyone he didn't like. Nebuchadnezzar thought he was more important than the Lord, but he was wrong. Before he knew it, he wasn't king any more, and nobody noticed him. He had to go and live outside in the fields with the wild donkeys, eating grass like a cow. His hair grew wild, and his nails were like the claws of an eagle.

Nebuchadnezzar learned the hard way that no human being is more important than the Lord. God is the most powerful of all. We are in His hands, and we can't go on as if He isn't there. We should thank the Lord every day for all He does for us.

Remember: We should not live as if God isn't there.

No one messes with God

June 9 Daniel 5

Although you knew all about the Lord, you didn't want to serve Him. (Dan. 5:22)

Belshazzar became king after King Nebuchadnezzar. He didn't pay any attention to the Lord either.

One day, he held a great feast. He took all the beautiful gold and silver cups from the temple. He and his guests drank from them, just to show they weren't afraid of the Lord. Then, suddenly, they saw a finger. Like a pen, the finger wrote on the wall: "Mene, Mene, Tekel, Upharsin." The king was so afraid that his face turned white. He didn't understand the words this finger wrote, so he called for Daniel. Daniel told him that the words meant: "The Lord has watched everything you do. He 'weighed' it. You have not listened to the Lord. You thought you could do what you wanted, and the Lord wouldn't mind. You laughed in His face and drank from the cups from His temple. Now you are going to find out, like Nebuchadnezzar before you, that there is only one God. And He is great and mighty."

That night Belshazzar died.

Remember: We must show respect for the ways of the Lord.

God brings His people back to life

June 10 Ezekiel 37

Then you will know that I am the Lord. (Ezek. 37:14)

The Lord promised to help His people again. He wouldn't let them stay in a foreign country forever. The Lord explained it to Ezekiel by taking him to a large valley. The valley was filled with human bones. "Do you think these bones can become living people again?" the Lord asked Ezekiel. "I don't know, but You know, Lord," Ezekiel answered. Then the Lord said, "Speak to these bones and say, 'Listen, dry bones, I am going to make you live again. Then you will know that I am the Lord.'"

As Ezekiel spoke, there was a rattling noise across the valley. The bones of each body came together, and every one settled in its right place. Then muscles and flesh formed over the bones, and skin covered the bodies. They looked like human beings again, but they weren't alive. Then the Lord sent His Spirit to breathe life into the bodies. They came to life and stood up. This story tells us what the Lord will do for His people. People who don't know Him are like dry bones. When the Lord becomes our God, he makes us come alive inside, just as He did with those bones. If we believe in Jesus, we will live with God forever.

Remember: A child of God lives with Him forever.

Water gives life to trees and fish

June 11 Ezekiel 47

If you believe in Me, I will give you rivers of living water. (John 7:38)

A desert is a lifeless place. Ezekiel says people who don't serve the Lord are like a desert. They are lifeless inside. The Lord showed Ezekiel in a dream that it won't stay that way forever. He dreamed that he was standing at God's temple in Jerusalem. All around the temple it was as dry as a desert. Suddenly, water started flowing from underneath the temple. Ezekiel walked beside this stream of water. It became deeper and deeper. Eventually, it was like a deep river. It flowed into the Dead Sea, which is in the middle of a desert.

Then the most amazing thing happened. As the water flowed into the Dead Sea, it was suddenly swarming with fish. Fruit trees started growing. Their leaves never turned brown, and there was always fruit on their branches. Ezekiel wondered what his dream meant. It meant that the Lord would bring His people out of exile. But it has another meaning as well. Jesus says that when the Holy Spirit enters the Lord's children, they will come alive and live for God.

Remember: A child of God should live for Him.

June 12 Ezra 1 & 8

God's people go back to Jerusalem

Then the exiles who came back worshiped the Lord. (Ezra 8:35)

Good news for the Jews! King Cyrus said they could go back home. They had been slaves in a foreign land long enough.

Ezra was a good man. He had to take his people back to Jerusalem and rebuild the city. They also had to build a temple for the Lord.

But what would happen when they reached Jerusalem? Strangers were living there. Surely these people wouldn't just let them take the land and build houses and a temple there? But the Lord helped them. The king gave Ezra a letter that told the people in Jerusalem to help Ezra and his men. No one would ignore that order.

Everybody who wanted to go back to Jerusalem had to meet at a river. There they asked the Lord to help them, and He took very good care of them. They had a safe journey, and now they were interested in only one thing—they wanted to obey the Lord and do His will.

Remember: We are so privileged to learn about God.

The temple is used for the first time

June 13 Nehemiah 1-9

Praise the Lord! (Neh. 9:5)

Ezra and his helpers struggled. It wasn't easy to build a temple if you didn't have the know-how and thieves kept stealing your bricks and tools.

At that stage, Nehemiah was working for the king of Persia. He heard how his people in Jerusalem were struggling, so he asked the king if he could go and help them. He knew a lot about building. The king gave him building materials and soldiers to protect them.

As soon as Nehemiah arrived in Jerusalem, he started building. The guards the king sent along protected him and his workmen. Now nobody could stop them from building their temple and a wall around the city. Once again, the Lord was taking care of His people.

Before long, the people had a place where they could worship the Lord again. They held a festival to celebrate the opening of their new temple. They were back in the land the Lord had given them, and they were overjoyed. Each one of us is privileged to have a church where we can worship the Lord without anybody trying to stop us.

Remember: We are privileged to serve in a church of our own.

Sing a song for the Lord

June 14 Psalms 134, 135, & 137

Praise the Lord, for He is good. (Ps. 135:3)

"It is much better to worship the Lord in a proper temple," the Jews said. With the Lord's help, they had a beautiful temple on Mount Zion where they could serve the Lord. They were very happy and sang praises to God.

"By the rivers of Babylon, we sat and wept. We thought about our temple on Mount Zion that had been destroyed. The people who held us prisoner made fun of us. They demanded, 'Sing us one of those songs of Jerusalem! Sing a joyful hymn for your temple.' But they knew it had been knocked down. How can we sing hymns for the Lord in a foreign land? But I will never forget you, Jerusalem. Every time I think of you, I will be joyful."

Now that they had their own temple again, they sang: "Praise Him, you who serve in the house of the Lord. Praise the Lord, for the Lord is good; glorify His wonderful name with music. Lift your hands in holiness, and bless the Lord. The Lord be praised, for He lives here in Jerusalem. Praise the Lord."

Remember: Never forget to tell others that the Lord is important.

Also help your enemies

June 15 Esther 1-2

Mordecai heard about the plot to kill the king. So he told Esther. (Esther 2:22)

Esther was so beautiful that King Xerxes asked her to marry him, and so Esther was crowned queen. She was very happy in the beautiful palace, but the king was not the same nationality as Esther. He was from Persia. Esther was a Jew, but the king didn't know that.

One day, two men decided to murder the king. Their job was to guard the door of the king's palace so it would be easy for them to kill him when he walked in the door. Mordecai, Esther's uncle, overheard the two guards talking about what they were planning to do. He went to Esther and told her. She informed the king and saved his life. The king never forgot it.

Even though the Persian people didn't like the Jews much, Mordecai did the right thing. He helped someone, even though that person didn't like him.

The Lord wants us to be kind to others, even if we don't always like them very much.

Remember: We should always help people, whether we like them or not.

June 16 Esther 3-6

Serving the Lord is worthwhile

Mordecai worked for the good of his people. (Esther 10:3)

Life did not always go well for Esther and the people of the Lord. The king put a bad man called Haman in charge of everything. He said everybody must bow before Haman to show him respect and serve him. Mordecai, Esther's uncle, refused. He served only the Lord.

Haman was very angry about this. He decided to kill Mordecai. He had a gallows made on which he was going to hang Mordecai. Mordecai went to Esther for help. They had a problem. The king didn't know that Esther was a Jew, so how could she explain to him why she wanted to help the Jews?

Esther was not only pretty, she was also smart. She prepared a delicious dinner for the king. He enjoyed it very much. Afterwards, he told Esther he would give her anything she asked for. Esther told him that Haman planned to kill Mordecai and reminded him that Mordecai was the one who had saved his life when he found out about the plot to murder him. The king was furious with Haman. He hanged Haman from the very gallows he had had built for Mordecai. Then the king gave Haman's job to Mordecai. It always pays to obey the Lord and do the right thing.

Remember: The Lord rejoices in our good actions.

The Devil tests Job

June 17 Job 1-2

When I was born, I came into the world with nothing. When I die I can take nothing with me. (Job 1:21)

There was a good man named Job. He served the Lord with all his heart, and God was good to him. One day, the Devil came to the Lord. The Lord asked him if he had seen how religious Job was. "Yes," said the Devil, "but not without reason. It's because You have always looked after him well. But take away everything he has, and then You will see." So the Lord answered the Devil: "All right, you may test him. Take whatever you want from Job, but don't harm him." So the Devil sent evil people to steal or break all of Job's belongings. Many terrible things happened to Job. He was left with nothing.

"Will Job be cross with the Lord, or not?" the Devil wondered. But Job wasn't angry with the Lord. He said, "I had nothing when I was born. I can take nothing with me when I die. The Lord gave me everything. Now, He has taken everything back. Praise the Lord!"

Job didn't get angry with the Lord, because He really loved Him.

Remember: Sometimes the Devil will also test us.

June 18 Job 2

How can someone be angry with God?

Should we accept only good things from the hand of God, and never anything bad? (Job 2:10)

The Devil thought Job would get angry with the Lord if he lost everything, but he was wrong. The Lord asked him again if he saw what a good man Job was. "Yes," said the Devil, "but a farm and other belongings are not so important. If You took away Job's health, that would be a different story. Job would be angry and forget all about You." The Lord said the Devil could give it a try. He made Job very sick. Big sores came out all over his body.

Job's wife said to him, "It doesn't look as if the Lord is your friend anymore. Tell Him you are angry with Him, and then you might as well die." Job answered, "Now, you are really being stupid. You don't know what you are saying. I was happy with all the good things the Lord gave me. So shouldn't I also be satisfied if things are going wrong now?"

The Devil was wrong. No matter how much Job suffered, he didn't do anything that would hurt the Lord. Job felt it was much better to be God's friend than to be rich or important.

Remember: Having a lot of money is not important.

Sometimes we don't understand the Lord

June 19 Job 4-5

You should be happy if the Lord shows you what to do, even if unpleasant things happen. (Job 5:17)

Does the Lord only love us when all goes well? What happens if things go wrong? Does this mean He has forgotten us? Job's friends thought so. They said to Job, "The Lord punishes those people He doesn't like. Look how you're suffering. He's not going to help you, that's for sure."

But Job's friends were wrong. If things are going well for us, or if we're rich, it doesn't necessarily mean that the Lord loves us. The Lord always loves us whatever our circumstances.

Eliphaz, one of Job's friends, did give Job some good advice: "If I were you, I would try talking to the Lord. I would ask Him why I am having such a hard time. Remember, the Lord is great. We can't always understand Him. So when the Lord lets something happen to you, it might be that He is trying to tell you something."

Job thought about it. He decided to speak to the Lord.

Remember: The Lord is so great that we can't always understand Him.

God is not a human being—
He is far greater

June 20 Job 38

Did you perhaps make the world, Job? (Job 38:4-5)

Job decided to talk to the Lord. He knew the Lord and how great and powerful He is. Although it wouldn't be like speaking to an ordinary person, Job decided that he would talk to God and ask Him why everything was going wrong for him. He obeyed the Lord, so why was he suffering? Job wanted God to answer him and give him an explanation.

The Lord did answer him. A loud voice came to him in a strong wind: "Job, do you think I don't know what I'm doing? Asking all these questions shows how little you understand. Now, I want to ask you a few questions: Who made the world? Who made the waves of the sea and the clouds? Who makes the sun rise in the morning and the moon at night?" Job had no answer. So the Lord went on: "Can you make the lightning strike? Or make the stars shine?" Job kept quiet.

As Job looked at creation, he knew that God is greater and more powerful than any human being.

Remember: The Lord is the creator of everything.

The Lord made it all

June 21 Job 39-41

Job, you criticize the Almighty, but do you have the answers? (Job 40:1)

The Lord went on talking to Job: "Job, see for yourself how wonderful the world is. The baby deer are born without any help. They run around in the open fields and don't need anyone to look after them. Who do you think cares for them? Look at the hawk soar in the sky and spread its wings. Are you the one who makes it fly, Job?" Then the Lord showed Job a crocodile. "Job," the Lord asked again, "can you catch a big crocodile with a fishing pole? Will you try to keep his mouth closed with your bare hands? Do you think the crocodile will tremble with fear when you come near him? Will you give a crocodile to little children to play with? You can try to fight a crocodile, Job, but you won't try it again. Who do you think made this fearless animal? Yes, I, the Lord, I made it. You are afraid of a crocodile that I made, but now you want to challenge Me?"

When we see the beautiful fields, the magnificent birds, the mighty mountains, and the red sun setting, we realize, like Job did, how wonderful God's creation is and why He is the Lord we want to serve.

Remember: The Lord created a beautiful world.

The Lord gives everything back to Job

June 22 Job 42

Now I know that the Lord can do anything. (Job 42:2)

The God we worship is great and mighty. Job learned this when God spoke to him. In the end, Job said: "Lord, what can I say? You are so wonderful and great. I am nothing. I know You can do anything. When You decide something should happen, it does. I have to admit that I wondered why things were going wrong for me, but now I know how wonderful You really are.

"I have heard how You made the earth. You told me how You make the hawk fly, how You keep the huge hippo alive and well although it only eats grass. You also made the lion that roars and the cruel crocodile. And there are so many other things, Oh Lord, that prove how wonderful You are.

"I'm ashamed, Lord, that I doubted You. Now I know better. I just knew what people told me about You before all this happened. Now I've seen You with my own eyes."

Then the Lord knew that Job loved Him very much. He gave Job back everything the Devil had taken away, and Job was happy for the rest of his life.

💡 **Remember:** Things happen in the Lord's time.

You can't run away from the Lord

June 23 Jonah 1-2

"You have Your own good reasons for what You do." (Jonah 1:14)

The Lord had a special job for Jonah. He had to go and tell the people of the big city Nineveh that God was not happy with them.

Jonah was afraid, so he boarded a ship that was going in the opposite direction from Nineveh. He thought he could get away from the Lord. That was a dumb idea! The Lord sent a violent storm. The ship creaked, and everyone on board thought it was going to sink. The sailors were terrified and started praying to their gods. All this time, Jonah was fast asleep in the hold. When the ship's captain found him there, he shouted at him: "How can you sleep at a time like this? Get up and pray to your God! Maybe He will help us."

Meanwhile the sailors cast lots to see who was the cause of the storm. They found out it was Jonah. "Who are you? What's your job?" they asked him. Jonah answered, "I worship the Lord who made the sea and the land." "So, what did you do wrong?" "I was disobedient. I didn't listen to the Lord," Jonah confessed. "Throw me into the sea, and it will become calm again." They did, and the storm died down, but it wasn't the end of the story.

Remember: We can't hide from the Lord.

June 24 Jonah 3

The Lord forgives our greatest sin

God saw they were sorry about their sins. He forgave them. (Jonah 3:10)

The sailors threw Jonah into the sea, but he didn't drown. God still had work for him to do, so He sent a fish to swallow Jonah. He was inside the fish for three days, and during this time he realized how disobedient he had been. Jonah asked the Lord to forgive him and, because he was really sorry, the Lord did. Three days later, the fish spat Jonah out onto the beach.

Jonah went to the evil city of Nineveh and talked to the wicked people there. He told them God was angry with them and was going to punish them. When the people of Nineveh heard this, they felt very badly. They begged the Lord to forgive them. They pleaded with Him not to let them die. The Lord saw that they were really sorry and that they wanted to do His will again. So He forgave them and let them live.

The Lord forgives us, too, if we are really sorry.

Remember: The Lord forgives us our sins if we are really sorry.

The Lord loves us

June 25 Jonah 4

"Lord, You do things for us we don't deserve. You love us." (Jonah 4:2)

When Jonah saw the Lord wasn't going to punish the people of Nineveh, he was upset because he'd told them they would be punished. He didn't think they'd pay attention to his warnings, but they had. They changed their evil ways, which was why the Lord forgave them.

Jonah took a walk. He sat down just outside the city on a hill. While he sat there, a plant suddenly started growing next to him. Jonah was pleased. The sun was hot, and the plant would give him some shade. Early the next morning, a worm ate through the stem of the plant, and the plant died. Jonah was furious. He'd have no protection from the burning sun.

The Lord asked Jonah, "Why are you so angry? You didn't make the plant grow. It's not really your plant. Now remember, I made the people of Nineveh just as I made the plant. They are like my own plant. I must worry about them and help them."

The Lord made us too. He loves us and wants only the best for us, and we must give Him our best.

Remember: We must do our best for the Lord.

The Lord will help

June 26 Psalm 130

Wait and watch for the Lord. (Ps. 130:7)

God's people knew the Lord would not forget them. He would come to them in a special way. In Psalm 130, the poet asks the Lord to come soon:

> "Lord, I'm all alone,
> I call out to You.
> Please hear my cry for help.
> Don't think of all the things I've done wrong;
> Please forgive me when I am bad.
> Then I can keep on being Your child.
> I trust You, Lord.
> I know You never lie.
> Like someone waiting for the sunrise,
> I wait for You.
> The Lord will not let us down.
> He can really help us.
> He will save us from our sins."

Remember: It hurts the Lord when we do wrong.

He died in our place

June 27 Isaiah 53

H*e carried all our sins.* (Is*a.* 53:4)

A boy called Andrew kept lots of chickens in a chicken coop. One day, the chickens scratched a hole under the fence and ran away. Andrew could have just let them go, but he didn't want to. They were his chickens. He started looking for them, and one by one, he brought them back.

The Lord also looks for us when we have strayed. We are often like the bad chickens who run away. We do things God doesn't like, but He doesn't just let us go. He comes looking for us.

Isaiah, the Lord's messenger, tells us how the Lord looks for us until he finds us. When we do bad things, we run away from God. But God has put our sins onto one Person—Jesus. We should have taken the punishment for our sins ourselves, but Jesus was punished in our place. He died so that we could be God's friends. God keeps on looking for us, because He loves us.

We need to love Jesus. He came to make us God's children again. We can go and tell everyone this. We can tell them how wonderful God is.

Remember: Jesus came to help us become God's children.

The Lord is not an idol

June 28 Jeremiah 10

Lord, there is no one like You! You are great, and Your name is full of power. (Jer. 10:6)

Jeremiah tells us how people made idols. They cut down a tree and carved an idol out of it with their hammers and chisels. They decorated it with gold and silver. Then they nailed it to the ground so it wouldn't fall over. They called the wooden statue "god", and they bowed before this "god" and worshiped it. But their god stood there like a helpless scarecrow. It couldn't talk to them. It couldn't even walk. It was just a piece of dead wood.

The God we worship is much greater and stronger than this. He made the earth. He is alive, and He takes care of us. He knows what we need and helps us with it. He is nothing like a dead idol.

Sometimes we think other things are more important than the Lord, and we spend all our time and energy on these things. That's wrong, because we are making idols of them, and nothing should be more important to us than the Lord.

Remember: Nothing should be more important than the Lord.

Come to me

June 29 Isaiah 1:18–20 & 55

Speak to the Lord while He is still near. (Isa. 55:6)

We know that the Lord never forgets His children. This is how He invites us to come to Him:

> Come to Me, so that we can make things better.
> No matter how bad your sins are, I can take them away.
> Even if you are red with sin, I will make you as white as snow.
> If you will just obey Me and let Me help you,
> I will take good care of you.
> But if you keep turning away from Me, you will pay for it!
> If you need something, come to Me.
> Even if you have nothing to give Me, come anyway.
> I will give you what you need, and it's all free.
> Don't waste your time on things that aren't really important.
> Come to Me, and I will give you eternal life.
> Ask while the Lord is still with you.
> Talk to Him while He is still near.

Remember: We shouldn't waste our time on things that aren't important.

June 30 Jeremiah 1

A messenger of the Lord

"O Lord, I'm too young." (Jer. 1:6)

Jeremiah was a priest in the temple. One day, the Lord said to him: "Even before you were born, I knew you. I decided then that you would be my special messenger."

Jeremiah answered, "O Lord, I am too young. I don't even speak well."

The Lord said, "Don't say you're too young. Go where I send you. Talk to the people. I will tell you what to say. Don't worry, I will be with you and take care of you." Then the Lord touched Jeremiah's mouth and said, "See, I have put My words in your mouth!"

From then on, the Lord was with Jeremiah wherever he went. He told Jeremiah what to say to the people. Jeremiah preached the message of God for many years.

So we mustn't say we're too young to work for the Lord. We can tell our friends and other people that the Lord is good. We can talk to our parents about Jesus. It makes God very happy when we talk to others about Him.

Remember: We should talk to our parents about Jesus.

People are excited, because Jesus is coming

July 1 Malachi 3-4

"People who listen to Me are like a special treasure to Me." (Mal. 3:17)

The people in the last book of the Old Testament were excited. They knew God was going to send Jesus to us, because He loves us so much. This is what Malachi says about it:

"The day will come when the Lord will punish wicked people and reward the good ones. He will come to those who serve Him. They will love being with Him. It will be like a flower enjoying the morning sun. He will heal the places where sin hurts them.

"The Lord will take good care of them, because they are His. He will treat them like a father who takes care of his children well. He will make His children feel safe, and they will be happy."

This is written in the last book of the Old Testament. The people were excited and happy. They were waiting for Jesus! When Jesus came, He was like the sun shining down warmly on people.

Jesus healed us from our sins. That's why we're happy, too. The Devil is no longer our master. We are free, cheerful, and happy, because Jesus loves us and takes care of us.

Remember: Jesus makes us children of God.

God talks to His people again

July 2 Luke 1

"God has come to help His people! He has not forgotten His promise to them." (Luke 1:54)

God did not forget His people. There were times in the Old Testament when people forgot about Him. They turned their backs on God, but God loves His people and never gave up on them.

In the Old Testament, God spoke to the people through His prophets. They promised that God would send Jesus to help all believers. The Devil would not stand a chance against Him.

What God had promised, happened when Jesus came to us. Mary, Jesus' mother, sang a song:

"God has come to help His children. He promised to be very good to us, and He has kept His promises. God is very powerful. He helps all who need help, and we are happy."

Mary sang this song because she knew that Jesus would bring people to God. We never have to feel alone. God is always with us, and Jesus can be our best friend.

Remember: Jesus can be our best friend.

John the Baptist is born

July 3 Luke 1

"John will bring you great joy and happiness." (Luke 1:14)

Zechariah and his wife, Elizabeth, were faithful believers who loved the Lord. They were sad, though, because they didn't have a baby, and they were very old. One day, Zechariah was in the temple. Suddenly, an angel stood before him. Zechariah nearly jumped out of his skin. But the angel said, "Don't be afraid! You will have a son. You must call him John. The Lord will use him to prepare the way for Jesus." Zechariah said, "How can this happen? I am an old man now." The angel Gabriel answered, "Since you don't believe me, you won't be able to speak until the child is born."

Elizabeth had a baby boy. The family came to congratulate her. "What are you going to name him?" they wanted to know. "John," answered Elizabeth. "But nobody in the family has that name," they said. "Let's go and ask Zechariah instead." Zechariah couldn't speak, so he wrote down, "His name is John." From that moment, he could speak again.

Zechariah had learned that, with God, nothing is impossible.

Remember: Nothing is impossible for the Lord.

An angel tells what God is going to do

July 4 Luke 1

"Mary, God has decided to bless you." (Luke 1:30)

Mary lived in Nazareth, a village in Galilee. She was engaged to Joseph. They were going to get married soon. Suddenly, Gabriel appeared to her. He said, "The Lord is with you!" Mary was very surprised. The angel went on. "Mary, you are going to have a son. You must call Him Jesus. He will be very important, because He is the Son of God."

Mary was confused and asked, "But how can I have a baby? I'm not married." The angel told her the Holy Spirit would give her the baby. That is why Jesus would be called the Son of God. "Nothing is impossible with God," he reminded her. So Mary said, "I am willing to do what God wants."

But Joseph was worried when he heard that Mary was pregnant. He didn't understand how it had happened. He knew he was not the father, so he didn't want to marry her anymore. But the angel of the Lord came to talk to him as well. He told Joseph that the Holy Spirit had given Mary the baby, and so they waited together for Jesus to be born.

Remember: We need to be ready to do what God asks.

Jesus is born

July 5 Luke 2

Jesus was born, and they wrapped Him snugly in strips of cloth. (Luke 2:7)

The Roman emperor at that time, Augustus, said all the people had to be counted. They had to go to the towns where their fathers were born and register. Joseph went to Bethlehem and took Mary with him. It was very close to the time when Jesus would be born.

When they finally arrived in Bethlehem, all the inns were full. They had to stay in a stable because it was time for the baby to be born.

Mary wrapped Him warmly in cloths. There wasn't even a crib for Him, so she laid Him in a manger.

Mary and Joseph were very happy. Jesus wasn't born in a palace, but in a humble place where ordinary people could come and see Him.

God loved human beings so much that He sent His Son for all of us—no matter who we are. It doesn't matter whether we're rich or poor, good-looking or not. Jesus came for us.

Remember: Jesus wants us to be His friends.

They called him Jesus and Immanuel

July 6 Matthew 1

"Mary will give birth to a son, and He will be called Immanuel." (Matt. 1:23)

Everything happened exactly the way the angel said it would. The baby was born, and Joseph named Him Jesus just as the angel had told him.

But Jesus had another name—Immanuel—that means "God is with us." Joseph couldn't help thinking back to a time long ago when God's people needed Him very much. Strangers wanted to hurt them and take their country away, but the Lord promised that these strangers wouldn't get what they wanted. The Lord would look after His people Himself. To prove His love for them, and to show that He was with them, a baby boy would be born. He would be called Immanuel.

Every time the Israelites were afraid of their enemies, all they had to do was remember the boy, Immanuel. He would remind them that they weren't alone. God was with them, and so was Jesus. He reminds us that God is always with us. We're never alone, because the Lord loves us.

Remember: God is always with us.

Mary thanks the Lord

July 7 Luke 1

"Oh, how I praise the Lord." (Luke 1:46)

Mary, Jesus' mother, wrote a poem to thank God for Jesus. This is what she said:

> "In my song, I want to say how great the Lord is.
> I'm excited and happy.
> God is going to take my sins away.
> He noticed me, Mary,
> even though I'm not important.
> He is so powerful;
> That is why He can do such awesome things for us.
> He takes such good care of people who serve Him.
> There is nothing He cannot do.
> If people don't like Him, He scatters them all over.
> But if people love Him, He takes good care of them.
> He keeps His promises.
> He is good to His people."

Remember: Jesus does what He promises.

The angels were happy

July 8 Luke 2

"Glory to God in heaven. And peace to everybody God loves," the angels sang. (Luke 2:14)

There were some shepherds near the place where Jesus was born. They were taking care of their sheep in the fields outside the village. Suddenly, an angel stood among them. It was like a bright light shining on them. They were frightened. "Don't be afraid," the angel said to them. "I have come to tell you something that will make you very happy. Jesus was born today. He is going to forgive all your sins. You will be God's special children. Go to the village. There you will find a baby lying in a manger."

Suddenly, a whole choir of angels joined the angel. They sang a lovely song. "Glory to God in heaven. Peace to everybody God loves."

Then the angels left. The shepherds said to each other, "Let's go to Bethlehem. Let's go and find the baby." They found Jesus and told everyone what the angels had told them. The people stood listening and were amazed. Later that night, the shepherds went back to their sheep. They sang and praised the Lord all the way there. This was their way of saying how great God is. They also thanked God for everything that happened that night.

Remember: Jesus helps us to become God's special children.

Not everybody is happy about Jesus

July 9 Matthew 2

Some wise men from the East asked, "Where is the newborn king of the Jews?" (Matt. 2:2)

One day, some wise men arrived in Jerusalem. They had seen a star that showed them a new king had been born. They didn't know exactly where, so they tried to find out if anybody knew where this new king was.

When King Herod heard that these men were looking for a new king, he was very upset. He had a meeting with the leaders and asked them about this special king. They said, "He will be born in Bethlehem."

Herod invited the wise men to his palace. "Go to Bethlehem and look for the child until you find him. Then come back and tell me so I can go and worship him, too," Herod told them. But Herod didn't want to take Jesus gifts. He wanted to kill Him.

The wise men found Jesus and gave Him the most beautiful gifts of gold, frankincense, and myrrh.

God told the wise men in a dream not to return to Herod, so they secretly took a different route home.

Remember: Jesus is the most important King of all.

Simeon and Anna are pleased to see Jesus

July 10 Luke 2

"Lord, I have seen how You will save Your people." (Luke 2:30)

Simeon lived in Jerusalem. He loved the Lord very much and was looking forward to the day when Jesus would come. God told him he would see Jesus before he died.

One day, the Lord's Holy Spirit told Simeon to go to the temple. The baby Jesus was there.

When Simeon saw the child, he picked Him up and took Him in his arms. He thanked the Lord: "Lord, now I can die in peace. I have seen Jesus. He is the One who will take away our sins. He will shine for us like a light in the darkness."

The things Simeon said surprised Joseph and Mary, so he told them, "Jesus will save many people. But many will also be punished, because they will refuse to listen to Him."

Anna, another woman who was also in the temple, came up to them. The Lord loved her. She served Him with all her heart. When she saw Jesus, she also thanked God. She couldn't stop talking about what Jesus would do for everybody.

Remember: Jesus takes our sins away if we believe in Him.

Jesus also goes to the temple

July 11 Luke 2

Jesus grew stronger and cleverer by the day. God and all who knew Him, liked Him very much. (Luke 2:52)

Every year, there was an important religious festival in Jerusalem. Jesus' parents always traveled there to celebrate this festival and took Jesus with them. When Jesus was twelve years old they were at the festival as usual.

After the celebrations were over, Jesus' father and mother and many other people started to go back home in a group. Nazareth was quite a way from Jerusalem. Jesus' parents didn't realize that their son had stayed behind in Jerusalem. They noticed later in the day that He wasn't around. They went back to Jerusalem to look for Him. They found Him in the temple talking with the priests. They were amazed that He was so smart.

Jesus' mother asked Him, "Why did You stay behind? We were worried about You." Jesus answered, "Why did you look for Me? You should have known I would be here. My Father is here." His parents didn't really understand what He meant. Jesus is the Son of God, and the temple was God's house. Jesus grew up to be strong and very smart.

Remember: Jesus is the Son of God.

God teaches Jesus everything

July 12 John 5

The Son does nothing by Himself. He does only what He sees His Father doing. (John 5:19)

How was it possible for Jesus to know everything? The Bible tells us that Jesus is God's Son. God taught Him everything, just like our parents teach us to do things.

This is the way God taught Jesus. He loved Jesus very much, and Jesus loved Him. That's why Jesus does everything exactly the way His Father showed Him. One of the most important things that His Father showed Him was how we can become God's children again.

God sent Jesus to tell us how we can become the children of God, so we need to know what Jesus says in the Bible. If we read our Bibles, we will know what God wants us to do.

Remember: Jesus came to show us how to be children of God.

John tells the people about Jesus

July 13 Matthew 3

"Prepare a path for the Lord. Make a straight road for Him!" (Matt. 3:3)

Jesus grew up. It was time for Him to start preaching to the people. God sent John the Baptist to prepare them for Jesus' coming.

John didn't preach in a synagogue or in the temple but in the fields beside the Jordan River. He ate locusts and wild honey.

John was a good preacher. His message was, "Turn from your sins and turn to God. It is time for Jesus, our King (Messiah) to come. Get ready for Him." People came from all over to hear John. They were glad that Jesus was coming, and they wanted to be ready for Him. They didn't want to sin anymore. John baptized them in the Jordan River.

Then John saw many of the Jewish leaders, the Pharisees, coming to be baptized. But they only pretended to serve the Lord. John spoke to them angrily. "It's no use pretending that you're good. You must live like people who love the Lord. God will treat a person well who lives the right way, but those who make the Lord sad will be punished."

Remember: Only do the things that will please God.

John baptizes Jesus

July 14 John 1

"Look! There is the Lamb of God who takes away the sin of the world!" (John 1:29)

One day, John was standing at the river baptizing people. Many people came to hear him preach. Then he saw Jesus coming towards him. Jesus asked John to baptize Him too. At first, John didn't want to baptize Jesus, but Jesus told him to do it. God wanted him to. Jesus wanted to show that He doesn't like sin at all. This was why John baptized people. Water makes people clean, and we are baptized because sin makes us dirty. We want to be washed clean from sin.

When John baptized Jesus, something suddenly came down from heaven. It looked like a dove, but it was the Holy Spirit. The Holy Spirit gave Jesus strength.

Then God spoke from heaven, saying, "This is my Son. I love Him very much. He makes Me very happy."

When this happened, John knew that Jesus was the Son of God. He told everybody. He also said, "Jesus will take our sins away."

Now Jesus was ready to tell people about God.

Remember: Jesus came to tell us about God.

The Devil wants to stop Jesus

July 15 Matthew 4

"Worship the Lord your God; serve only Him." (Matt. 4:10)

After Jesus was baptized, He went into the desert with the Holy Spirit. While He was there, the Devil tried to make Jesus sin.

Jesus didn't have anything to eat for a very long time. He was very hungry. The Devil said to Him, "If You are God's Son, change these stones into loaves of bread." But Jesus said, "No, food is not that important. It is more important to listen to every word of God."

Then the Devil took Jesus to the temple. They went up on the roof. He said, "If You are the Son of God, jump off! Surely the angels will help you so you won't get hurt." Jesus said to the Devil, "The Bible says we should not test God."

The Devil tried a third time. He took Jesus to a very high mountain. The Devil showed Jesus the whole world from there. He said, "I will give it all to You, if You will only kneel down and worship me." Jesus said, "Get out of here, Satan!" The Bible says we should pray to God and no one else. Then the Devil went away, defeated.

Remember: The Devil couldn't do anything against Jesus.

The Devil wants to stop you, too

July 16 Matthew 7; Luke 13

"Follow the narrow road that leads to the right door." (Matt. 7:13-14)

Someone once asked Jesus what sort of people would go to heaven. Jesus said, "Try your best to serve the Lord. Some people only try for a little while. Then they give up and start listening to the Devil. They won't go to heaven."

We can choose which way we want to go—to keep trying even though it's hard or to give up because that's easier.

It's not always easy to listen to the Lord and to do the right thing. This is like walking along a difficult road. It might be hard, but this road takes us to heaven. If we don't listen, and choose the easy road, we won't find the door to heaven. That will please the Devil! He wants to stop us from taking the road to heaven—but we're not going to let him!

Remember: Don't listen to the Devil.

Whose side are you on?

July 17 Matthew 12

Jesus said, "Anyone who isn't working with Me is actually working against Me." (Matt. 12:30)

Once, some people brought a man to Jesus. He had a demon inside him so he couldn't talk or see. Jesus chased the demon out of the man, and he was healed.

The Jewish leaders, the Pharisees, didn't like Jesus. When they heard how Jesus had ordered the demon out of the man, they said Jesus must be a friend of the Devil, and that's why the Devil listened to Him. Jesus told them they were making a big mistake. "I threw out the demon," Jesus said. "This means that I'm not on the Devil's side."

"I beat the Devil," Jesus went on. "God's Spirit gives Me the power over demons, and that's why the Devil runs away when I speak. If a strong man lives in a house, and you want to break into his house, you have to tie him up first. I overpowered the Devil. I'm in charge, not the Devil. If you're not on My side, you're against Me."

Remember: Jesus has defeated the Devil.

We shouldn't be afraid of the Devil

July 18 Matthew 8

The demons started screaming at Him, "Why are You bothering us, Son of God?" (Matt. 8:29)

One day, Jesus walked past a graveyard. Two men who lived in the graveyard ran up to Jesus. They had demons inside them, and everybody was afraid of them because they were very dangerous. When they saw Jesus, they stopped in their tracks and shouted, "What do you want, Son of God? Have you come to hurt us?"

A large herd of pigs was nearby. "Please, don't send us to hell. Let us go into those pigs and live inside them," the demons begged. "All right, go!" Jesus told them. So the demons went into the pigs. The pigs started running wildly down the hillside and into the sea. They all drowned.

The herdsmen, who looked after the pigs, ran into town. They told everybody what had happened and that Jesus had healed the two dangerous men. But the townspeople were bad. The two men weren't their problem. They didn't care about them; they were just worried about their pigs. They chased Jesus away. They wanted to get rid of Him!

Remember: Always choose Jesus.

Jesus chooses His special friends

July 19 Luke 5

"From now on, you'll be fishing for people!" (Luke 5:10)

One day, Jesus was walking beside the lake. Many people crowded around to hear Him preach. Jesus asked some fishermen if He could sit in their boat. He used it as a kind of pulpit. Jesus sat in the boat and told the crowds about God. When He had finished, He said to a fisherman called Simon, "Thank you for letting Me use your boat. Now, take it out to the middle of the lake and let your nets down." Simon said, "We've been fishing all night, and we haven't caught a thing, but I'll try again." He did as Jesus said, and he and his friends caught so many fish that they had to load some onto a second boat.

Everyone realized how wonderful the Lord was. Simon went down on his knees before Jesus. "Lord, I have so many faults. I am sinful. It is better if You go away from me." But Jesus answered, "Don't be afraid. I want you to help Me. You must go and tell people about Me. Just like you caught those fish, you must catch people for Me." When they got back to shore, Simon left his boat and followed Jesus. They became good friends.

Remember: Jesus loves us even if we sometimes make mistakes.

Jesus invites everybody

July 20 Matthew 22

"Tell everybody who has been invited that the meal is ready." (Matt. 22:4)

Jesus said heaven is like a feast. A king once invited people to a feast but, when everything was ready, the people who had been invited didn't come. They were too busy doing their own thing: one had gone to his farm, and another said he had too much work. The king sent messengers to tell them, "The meal has been cooked. Everything is ready. Hurry!" But they were rude to the king's messengers and chased them away. The king was very angry. He sent his army to punish these people.

Then the king said, "Go out and invite everyone you see to the feast." Many people came. The hall was filled with guests.

Do you know who the first group of people are—those who were invited but didn't come? They are people who think they are so important that they don't need the Lord. They don't really love Him, and the Lord will punish them.

The others who came to the feast are the people who listen to the Lord. They want to do what He says. That's why they come when He calls. They aren't disobedient, and someday they'll be at God's feast in heaven.

Remember: Jesus invites everybody to be His children.

Jesus also invites children

July 21 Mark 10

"Let the children come to Me. Don't stop them!" (Mark 10:14)

One day, when Jesus was talking to the people, some parents brought their children to Him. They wanted Jesus to speak to the children, to touch them and bless them. But Jesus' friends told them not to bother Jesus. He was busy with the grown-ups. When Jesus heard this, He wasn't pleased with His friends. He loves children, so He said, "Don't keep the children away from Me. They must come to Me. God loves children."

Jesus looked at the grown-ups and said, "If you want to serve the Lord, you must be like children. A child listens to what his father or mother says.

"You must also listen to what the Lord says," Jesus told them. "When someone helps one of God's children, God is very happy, and He will help that person. But if someone should hurt one of God's children, God will punish that person. It would be better for that person to tie a heavy stone around his neck and jump into the sea."

It is true. God loves children.

Remember: Jesus loves little children in a special way.

Even if you hide, Jesus still invites you

July 22 Luke 19

Jesus came to look for people. He wants to make them children of God. (Luke 19:10)

A rich man called Zacchaeus lived in Jericho. The people didn't like him because he was a tax collector, and they said he took more money from them than he was supposed to. One day, Jesus came past. Zacchaeus tried to see Him, but Zacchaeus was short and couldn't see over people's heads. Zacchaeus decided to run ahead and climb a tree beside the road. When Jesus came to the tree, He suddenly stopped and looked up: "Zacchaeus, come down right now! I'm going to visit your house today." Zacchaeus climbed down quickly. He was very happy.

The people were angry with Jesus. Why did He choose to go to the home of a bad man? But Jesus changed Zacchaeus's whole life. Zacchaeus said, "I will give back to everybody the money I took from them. I will even give them extra." Jesus said to Zacchaeus, "Now, you are My friend." Jesus also spoke to the people who wondered why He had visited a man like Zacchaeus: "I came to find sinners. You know that they need God, too. I have to help them to become God's children."

Jesus invites us all to be His friends.

Remember: Jesus wants to help bad people become God's friends.

Jesus also invites people others don't like

July 23 John 4

"If you drink the water I give you, you will never be thirsty again." (John 4:14)

One day, Jesus and His friends had walked a long way. They were tired. When they came to a well, they sat down beside it to rest. Then Jesus' friends went into the village to buy some food.

A woman came to the well. She was not a Jew like Jesus, but a Samaritan. The Jews didn't like the Samaritans. They didn't even talk to each other. But Jesus was never rude. He asked the woman for some water. She was very surprised. "I am a Samaritan. Why are you asking me for a drink of water?" Jesus said, "I can also give you water. If you drink it, you will never be thirsty again." Jesus was not talking about real water, but about spiritual water.

You can describe someone who wants to know God as "thirsty" for God. Jesus can take that "thirst" away. He can teach that person about God.

Remember: Jesus teaches us who God is.

Don't make the wrong choice, like the rich young man

July 24 Mark 10

"Then come back and follow Me." (Mark 10:21)

We have to choose if we want to be Jesus' friend or not. If we choose to be His friend, we need to do what He asks us.

There was a rich young man who came to Jesus and asked, "What do I have to do to be Your friend?" Jesus answered, "You know what God wants. He told us that in the Ten Commandments." The young man said, "I've obeyed these commandments since I was a child."

Jesus liked him very much, and He said to the young man, "Go and sell all you have. Give the money to people who need it. Then come, follow Me." The man's face grew sad. He loved everything he owned more than he loved Jesus. He would rather stay and keep his riches than go with Jesus.

We have a choice, too. We can choose to be Jesus' friend and do whatever makes Him happy.

Jesus loves us. He asks us to be His friend.

Remember: Jesus wants to be our special friend.

Jesus makes us happy

July 25 John 3

John said, "Jesus must become greater, and I must become less." (John 3:30)

It is great being Jesus' friend. The Bible tells us it's almost like going to a wedding. We go to the reception where the delicious cake and the other good things to eat and drink are. But we have to wait there until the bride and groom arrive. It may feel like a long, boring wait, but when the bride and groom finally arrive everyone is very glad. Then the feasting can start, and we don't have to wait anymore.

Jesus makes our lives as enjoyable as a wedding. If He isn't there, it is boring. But when we become His friends, then we enjoy life. It's as if the groom is there. At a wedding, we like to do things for the groom. We feel special if he asks us to help him. When we are Jesus' friends, we really feel special. We want to do what He asks. We want to make Him happy.

Remember: We are special to the Lord.

The Lord makes everything new for His friends

July 26 John 3

"Unless you are born again, you cannot be the Lord's child." (John 3:3)

When a baby is born, he is very tiny. His parents feed him and take care of him. He learns to walk and play. Later on, he goes to school. But everything starts when the baby is born.

Jesus says we also have to be born if we want to be God's children. We must be born again, or reborn. Everything starts there.

The Holy Spirit helps us so that we can be born a child of God. This means that God becomes our Father in spirit. We then have both an earthly father and a heavenly Father.

Just as a baby learns to eat and walk, we can learn from God how to be His children. He will teach us to do what pleases Him. Just as the parents of a little baby teach him everything, God teaches us, His children, everything. That's why Jesus said to Nicodemus, "Unless you are born again, you cannot be the Lord's child." The Holy Spirit helps us to be God's children in spirit. We should thank God that we can be His children.

Remember: We should thank God for the privilege of being His children.

Jesus invites us through the Bible

July 27 Matthew 13

"A *farmer went out to plant some seed ...*"(Matt. 13:3)

One day, a farmer went out to plant some seeds. As he scattered them across his field, some seeds fell on a path. The birds came and ate them. Other seeds fell between stones, where the dirt wasn't very deep. The plants came up quickly. But they soon wilted in the hot sun, because the roots were too small. Other seeds fell among thorns. The seeds tried their best to grow, but the thorns grew all over them. Other seeds fell on good soil. They grew well. They gave the farmer a good crop.

Jesus says the same thing happens with people who hear about Him. Like the seeds that fell on the path, some people hear Jesus' words, but they don't listen. The Devil takes the words away. Others hear what Jesus says. For a while they're excited, but they quickly forget all about it like the seeds that fell among the stones. Then there are the people who are like the seeds that fell among the thorns. They listen to what Jesus says, but the minute something goes wrong in their lives they forget all about Him.

But the people who listen to Jesus and who do what He tells them are like the seeds that fell in good soil. The words of Jesus grow well in them.

Remember: Listen to the Bible and do what it says.

Jesus uses us like a light to invite others

July 28 Matthew 5

"Let your good deeds shine like a light for all to see." (Matt. 5:16)

We should not be ashamed to be God's children. We should never try to hide it.

A child of God is like a light in the world. When we switch on a light, everyone can see. If it's dark, we need a flashlight. And what's the use of taking a flashlight along and keeping it in our pocket? The smart thing to do would be to take it out, switch it on, and let its light shine out. God says a Christian is like a light. A Christian should tell other people about Jesus. We should shine like a light for all to see. If we are Christians, we shouldn't hide that fact.

A Christian is also like a mountain. A mountain cannot hide. And a Christian cannot hide. People should be able to tell by a person's life that he or she loves Jesus. So we must be friendly, good, and helpful and love our friends and other people. We must copy Jesus' example. Then we will be like a light that shows other people how great God is.

Remember: We must be the light of God for other people.

Show others it's great to serve Jesus

July 29 Matthew 5

"You are the salt of the earth." (Matt. 5:13)

If food doesn't have any salt in it, it has no flavor. In the old days, salt was even more important than it is today. In those days, people didn't have refrigerators. They put salt on the food so it wouldn't go bad and could be stored for a long time.

But sometimes the salt became lumpy, or it tasted bad. Then it couldn't be used with food.

The Bible says we are the salt of the world. We have to work for God in this world. We need to tell people about Him and how wonderful it is to belong to Him. That way, we can make their lives better because they will get to know the Lord. Just as salt stops food from going bad, we will help them not to become bad.

If we live like Jesus' children, then we are like salt. But if we do things the Lord doesn't like, then we become like the salt that is useless, and we hurt the Lord.

Remember: We need to be like salt for other people.

It's nice to be Jesus' friend

July 30 Matthew 13

"If you want something of value, you will take all your money and buy it." (Matt. 13:46)

To know Jesus is more important than anything else.

Jesus told a story about a treasure that was buried in a field. A man heard about it. He was very excited and wanted this treasure so badly that he sold all his things. He used the money to buy the land to get the treasure.

This treasure is like being Jesus' friend. Nothing is more important than that. That is why we have to give everything to be His friend.

To be a friend of Jesus is great. Not to be His friend is terrible. Jesus said it's like a fisherman who catches lots of fish in a big net. He keeps the good fish and throws away the rest. God does the same thing. If we serve the Lord, we are the good fish whom He keeps with Him. But if we lead bad lives and don't love the Lord, He will make us go away from Him.

There's nothing more important than being Jesus' friend.

Remember: To know Jesus is more important than anything else.

Jesus wants to be our best friend

July 31 Matthew 11

"It is good to be the Lord's child and to live the way He wants you to." (Matt. 11:29)

People often think it's difficult to be God's child. But Jesus came to show us that it's easy. It's fun to be Jesus' friend.

Listen to what Jesus told the people: "You don't need to go to school to know that the Lord loves you. Your parents can tell you Jesus loves you very much." That's easy to understand.

Jesus also says, "When you're afraid, come to Me and tell Me all about it. If you're sad, tell Me. If you don't know what to do, ask Me. I will help you." The Lord wants to be like a good friend to us. He wants to be with us, and He wants to help us.

It's great to have God with us all the time. He is the best friend we could ever have.

Remember: Jesus is with us and wants to help us.

August 1 Mark 9

Children are very important to God

"Anyone who wants to be important to God must be prepared to help other people with everything." (Mark 9:35)

One day, Jesus and His friends were together at home. He asked them what they had been doing all day. They were ashamed to tell Him, because they had been arguing about which of them was the most important. Jesus knew this, so He said, "Do you know who is the most important to God? It is someone who wants to help others. Someone who doesn't think only of himself. He or she thinks of others and likes doing what the Lord wants. God wants everyone to be kind to one another."

Jesus called a small child to come over to Him. "Someone who loves a child also loves Me. Christians should care for little children. This is what God wants. If you hurt even one of these little ones, God will punish you."

When we are Jesus' children, we don't have to worry. Even if something happens that scares us, we just need to remind ourselves that Jesus loves us and will watch over us. We don't need to be afraid, because we are very important to the Lord.

💡 **Remember:** As Jesus' children, we don't have to be afraid.

Jesus helps a little girl who believed

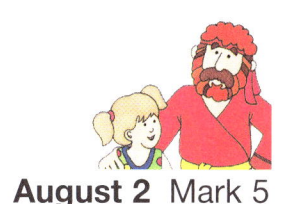

August 2 Mark 5

Jesus said, "Get up, little girl!" And the girl immediately stood up and walked around. (Mark 5:41-42)

An important man called Jairus came hurrying to Jesus one day. "My daughter is very sick. I think she's going to die," he said. "Please help her. Please come and make her well again. Don't let her die." While Jesus was on His way there, Jairus's friends brought this message: "Your little girl is dead. There's no use troubling Jesus now."

Jesus heard them. He comforted Jairus. "Don't be sad. Just trust Me." Then Jesus went to Jairus's house. There were many people there crying bitterly. Jesus went into the house and asked, "Why all this crying? The little girl isn't dead. She is only sleeping." The people thought, "How stupid of Him!" And they laughed. Couldn't He see she was dead?

Jesus told everybody to leave the house. Only the little girl's parents and Jesus' friends stayed with Him. He walked over to the little girl and took her hand. Then He said, "Little girl, get up!" And the girl immediately got up and walked around. Her parents gave her something to eat. The people couldn't believe it. Jesus is our friend, too, if we believe in Him.

Remember: Jesus helps His friends.

Jesus also helps grown-ups who believe

August 3 John 9

"One thing I know: I was blind, and now I can see!" (John 9:25)

One day, a man who was born blind sat begging for money to buy food. Jesus was walking past, but He saw him and stopped. He put a little mud on the man's eyes. "Go and wash your eyes in the pool of Siloam," He told the man.

The man did as Jesus said, and suddenly he could see! The people asked, "But isn't this the blind man who always sits here begging?" "Yes, I am that man!" he kept saying. "But how is it that you can see now? What happened?" they wanted to know. So the man told them how Jesus made him see again.

There were people who didn't like Jesus—the Pharisees. They were angry when they found out that Jesus had healed the blind man. They were jealous. But the blind man kept telling everyone that Jesus was a good man—the Pharisees were wrong.

When the man saw Jesus again a little later, he knelt down before Him and said, "You are really the Son of God." And so he became Jesus' friend.

Remember: Jesus is our Lord. We should worship Him.

Trust the Lord

August 4 Luke 5

Jesus said, "Your sins are forgiven." (Luke 5:20)

Jesus healed many people. They came from everywhere and crowded around Jesus wherever He was. One day, people came to the house where Jesus was, carrying a paralyzed man on a stretcher. They tried their best to get him to Jesus, but they couldn't push through the crowd so they went up onto the roof. They took off some tiles and lowered the sick man into the room below. They put him down right in front of Jesus. When Jesus saw the faith they had in Him, He said to the man, "I forgive you all your sins."

Before Jesus could say another word, the Pharisees said, "Who does this man think He is? Everyone knows only God can forgive sins." Jesus said, "Anybody can say he forgives someone. But not everybody is powerful enough to do it. I'll show you how powerful I really am." Then Jesus turned to the paralyzed man and said, "Stand up, take your stretcher, and go home." And right there, as everyone watched, the man did just that. He was overjoyed. He could not stop thanking the Lord. Jesus had proved again how powerful He really is.

Trust the Lord. He can do whatever He promises us.

Remember: Nobody is as strong as Jesus.

August 5 John 15

Our strength is from the Lord

"Those who stay near Me and I near them, they will do as I ask." (John 15:5)

One day, Jesus told a story to explain what it meant to be His friend.

He said He is like a fruit tree. His Father, God, is like the farmer who has to care for the tree. We are like the branches of the fruit tree. The farmer also takes care of the branches. He cuts them back so that they can bear good fruit. He cuts off every branch that doesn't yield any fruit.

A branch that isn't part of the tree can't bear fruit, can it? A person who is not part of Jesus cannot do what He says, either. When a branch is attached to a tree, it gets its strength from the tree. Then lots of fruit can grow on it. Without the tree, the branch can't do anything. It's the same with us. We should be Jesus' good friends. We shouldn't let go of Him. We have to be like a branch on a tree. Then He will make us strong. He will help us to do things that make God happy. We can pray and ask Him to help us, and He will.

We should be Jesus' branches. Unless branches are part of the tree, they're useless. We should stay close to Jesus, too.

Remember: Always stay close to Jesus.

Jesus takes care of us

August 6 Matthew 6

"First live for God. Then He will give you all you need." (Matt. 6:33)

The Lord doesn't want us to worry too much. We need to remember that He will take care of us. Jesus explained it by saying:
"Look at the birds. They don't plant. They don't build barns to store food. So how do they stay alive? The Lord feeds them."

We are more important to the Lord than a bird, so He will take even better care of us. God doesn't want us to worry too much. It isn't good for us.

Look at the wild flowers that grow in the fields. They don't make themselves clothes. Yet, they are beautiful. They are sometimes prettier than the most expensive clothes you can buy in a store. Do you know who dresses the flowers? The Lord Himself does. He takes care of them.

We're more important than flowers, and God will take even better care of us.

Our Father in heaven knows what we need. He will take care of us. We shouldn't worry. All the Lord wants us to do is to listen to Him. We must be good because we are His children, and He will give us all we need.

Remember: We shouldn't worry. The Lord provides.

Jesus takes care of us— Just trust Him

August 7 Matthew 8

Jesus said, "Go on home. What you have believed has happened." (Matt. 8:13)

Once a soldier came to Jesus for help. This soldier was in charge of many other soldiers.

He said to Jesus, "Please help. One of my men is in so much pain he can hardly walk."

Jesus said, "All right, I will come."

The soldier answered, "Lord, You are too important to come to my house. Just say the word, and the man will be healed. I know how it works. Among my men, I'm the important one. They do what I tell them. I give the orders, and they listen when I speak. You also just say the word, and it will happen."

What the man said surprised Jesus. He said, "This man really trusts Me. People like him are friends of God." Then Jesus said to the soldier, "You can go home. What you believed has happened." The sick man was healed as soon as Jesus spoke. We can trust God, too.

Remember: We can trust the Lord.

Jesus feeds many people

August 8 John 6

"I am the bread of life. Those who eat this bread will never be hungry again." (John 6:35)

Jesus and His friends were at the Sea of Galilee. Crowds gathered on the shore. Many people there were hoping that Jesus would heal them. After a while, the people started getting hungry. Jesus asked one of His friends, "Philip, where can we buy bread for all these people?" Philip replied, "I don't know. We'd need lots of money to buy food for all these people." Meanwhile, one of Jesus' other friends came up to Him and said, "There's a little boy here with a little food. He has five bread rolls and two dried fish. But it's not nearly enough for all these people."

Then Jesus said, "Tell everyone to sit down on the grass." Thousands of people sat down. Then Jesus took the bread. He prayed, giving thanks to God for the food. Then He started passing around the bread and the fish. The people ate, and there was more than enough food for every single one of them. There were even leftovers!

This is how Jesus takes care of us. He not only gives us food to eat. He also helps us to be children of God forever.

Remember: Jesus also provides our food.

August 9 Luke 12

You can't do anything without the Lord

The most important thing in a person's life is not how much money he has. (Luke 12:15)

One day, two brothers came to Jesus. They were arguing bitterly. Their father had died, and they had to divide his money between them. They asked Jesus to help them. But Jesus saw they weren't really interested in Him, only in the money.

So Jesus told them a story. There was once a rich man with a big farm. He always had very good crops. In fact, his barns were overflowing. "What shall I do now?" he wondered. "I know. I'm going to pull my barns down and build bigger ones. Then I'll have enough room to store up everything I own. And I won't need anybody anymore. I can sit back and enjoy life, because I am a rich man." The Lord said, "You fool! Tonight you are going to die in your bed. And what will you have then? What will the things you hoarded mean to you? You can't take them with you."

Jesus told this story to teach us that it's no good having lots of things if we forget about God. It's much better to work hard and make Him happy. Then we'll be able to enjoy all the wonderful things He gives us.

Remember: Jesus is much more important than money.

We should always thank Jesus for taking care of us

August 10 Luke 17

He went to Jesus and thanked Him very much. (Luke 17:16)

One day, Jesus came across ten men. They were all very sick. They had leprosy. The townspeople chased them out of their town, because they were scared of catching the disease. The men didn't come close to Jesus but cried out to Him from a distance, "Jesus, please help us." "All right," Jesus said. "Go into town and show the people you aren't sick anymore." On the way to the village, their sickness vanished.

Only one man turned back when he saw he was healed. He came back to Jesus to thank Him. He shouted, "Praise God, I am healed!" Then he lay facedown on the ground at Jesus' feet, because he was so grateful. Jesus asked him, "Where are the other men who were healed? Doesn't even one of them want to thank God?" Then Jesus told this man, "You can go home now. Today you were not only healed. You saw how good God is. From now on, you are God's friend."

We should always thank God for all He does for us.

Remember: Thank the Lord for everything He does for you.

We should do what Jesus asks

August 11 Luke 14

Jesus said, "No one can become My friend without giving up everything for Me." (Luke 14:33)

The Lord is our friend, and He is good to us, so we should be careful not to make Him sad.

To build a house the builders need lots of bricks, cement, and a roof. Without bricks and cement, a builder can't build a house. People would laugh at him if he tried. They might say, "He wants to build a house, but he doesn't have any bricks." Jesus doesn't want us to be like that—saying we want to be His friends and then doing nothing about it. It's like wanting to build a house without bothering to get any bricks.

What should we do to be Jesus' friend?

- First of all, we have to want to be His friend and to trust Him.
- Then, we need to ask what He wants us to do. We will find that answer in the Bible.
- Sometimes, God will ask us to do something we don't really feel like doing, but we must be obedient and do it.

These things are like "bricks" that build our friendship with Jesus.

Remember: The Bible teaches us God's will.

Talk is cheap

August 12 Matthew 21

"Son, go out and work on the farm today." (Matt. 21:28)

Going to church is important, but what we do when we're there is even more important.

We can sit in church and listen to what the minister is saying but ignore it. We can sing a beautiful song to God but not mean it. Then going to church isn't worthwhile. Going to church only works if we want to listen to the Lord and do what He asks.

Jesus told a story about this: Once there was a man who had two sons. He said to one of them, "Son, please go and work on my farm today." "No," the boy said. "I don't feel like it." Later, he felt badly about it. So, he went out and worked on the farm.

Then the father called his other son. He asked him the same thing. "Yes, father, I will go," he said. But he didn't.

Which son did what the father wanted? The first one, of course.

It doesn't matter if we just say we want to serve God. We have to do it. If the Lord asks us to do something, we must be willing to do it.

Remember: Listen to the Lord.

Helping others is important to the Lord

August 13 Matthew 25

"If someone does what the Lord wants, he will be with God in heaven forever." (Matt. 25:46)

One day, the Lord will decide who goes to heaven and who doesn't. We call this the final judgment. Jesus will divide all the people into two groups. He will say to one group, "God wants you to be in heaven with Him." Do you know why? The Lord gives the answer: "I was hungry, and you fed Me. I was thirsty, and you gave Me a drink of water. I was sick, and you gave Me medicine." When they ask, "Lord, when did we do this for You?" Jesus will answer, "When you help anyone who is My child, you also help Me. If you give someone who isn't important a glass of water, it's like giving it to Me."

To the other group He will say, "Go away from Me. You are the Devil's children. I was thirsty, and you wouldn't give Me anything to drink. I was hungry, and you didn't even give Me a bite to eat." They will be surprised and ask, "When did we see You and not help You?" Jesus will then say, "You weren't willing to help the most unimportant of My children, so you don't want to help Me, either." We should always help others.

Remember: We should always help others.

What you do shows what you are

August 14 Matthew 7

"A healthy tree produces good fruit, and an unhealthy tree produces bad fruit." (Matt. 7:17)

There are people who say they are the Lord's children, but they do wicked things. They don't love God. Jesus says we have to watch out for these people.

Jesus gave the following example. Only peaches grow on a peach tree. So how will you know if the tree in your garden is a peach tree? By its fruit. If you have a tree that doesn't give you peaches, you'll know it's not a peach tree. You'll be able to tell by its fruit what kind of tree it is.

It's the same with people. Watch what they do. Do they love one another? Watch what they say. Are they friendly, and are they kind to children? If so, we can tell they are good people. But if a person does and says bad things all the time, then we know that person is like a tree that is no use to anybody. We should never do wrong things but should always try to please the Lord. We should try to grow good fruit in our lives.

Remember: God's children should be friendly.

We need to help each other

August 15 Luke 10

"Go and do the same." (Luke 10:37)

The Bible says we should help our "neighbor." Who is our "neighbor"? Jesus told a good story to explain it. One day, a man was traveling from one town to another. Robbers attacked him. They beat him up and took all his clothes and money. They left him lying in the road, half dead. Two religious people passed by at different times. They saw the man but neither of them helped him. One of them even crossed to the opposite side of the road.

Then a Samaritan came along. The Jews didn't like Samaritans one bit. They wouldn't even talk to a Samaritan. He saw the man lying there by the side of the road and felt very sorry for him. He knelt down beside him and helped him. He put ointment on his wounds and bandaged them. Then he took the man to the nearest inn, where he could be looked after. He asked the innkeeper to care for the man, and he paid the bill. "If this isn't enough, I'll pay the rest when I come back," the Samaritan said.

Who did the right thing? The Samaritan, of course. We should help others too, whether we like them or not. If people need our help, we must give it to them.

Remember: Even if we dislike someone, we should be prepared to help him.

We need to serve one another

August 16 John 13

"You ought to wash each other's feet." (John 13:14)

In Jesus' time, people didn't have cars. They had to walk. They didn't sit on chairs and eat at a table, either. They lay sideways on benches around a table. They always washed their feet before a meal. It was the servants' job to wash people's feet.

Jesus and His friends were getting ready for supper. Suddenly, Jesus got up and brought a basin and a towel. He started washing His friends' feet. His friends were surprised. It just wasn't done—an important person washing other people's feet! When Jesus came to Peter, Peter protested, "Lord, You are not going to wash my feet." Jesus answered, "Well, if you don't want Me to wash your feet, then you are not My friend." Peter quickly said, "Then wash my hands and face as well, Lord." "No, only your feet," Jesus answered. Jesus wanted this to be a lesson to His friends. We should never think about our own importance. In church, we should be willing to do the unimportant little jobs for the Lord. If He needs us, no matter what it is for, we should do it.

Remember: We need to be ready to do anything, however unimportant, for Jesus.

We should not hurt each other

August 17 Matthew 5

"Leave everything, and go and make your peace with your brother." (Matt. 5:24)

The Lord doesn't like us to fight. He says fighting is almost like killing a person. It's not good to say things to our friends like, "You jerk!" or to swear at them or spread rumors about them.

This is what Jesus says. "God is angry with people who talk about others. If we're angry and feel like hurting someone, God gets upset with us."

If we are in church and remember that a friend is angry with us, then we should get up and go and make peace with that person. Afterwards, we'll enjoy being in church much more.

We shouldn't look for trouble. Sometimes people bother us, but we need to ignore it and not think, "I'll pay you back. Just wait!"

The Lord wants us to keep the peace. He doesn't want us to fight. We should try being friendly with people who are looking for trouble, and in the end they won't have any excuse to start a fight.

Remember: Don't look for trouble. Find peace.

Forgive each other

August 18 Matthew 18

"You must forgive one another." (Matt. 18:35)

One day there was a king who had lots of different farms. He had a foreman on one of these farms. The king decided to bring his accounts up-to-date. He asked the foreman to help him. Then the king noticed that this man owed him millions of dollars. He couldn't pay it back. In those days a man who owed that kind of money was sold, together with his belongings, to pay off his debts. The king said this man had to be sold. He begged the king, "Oh sir, please be patient with me. I will pay it all back." The king felt sorry for him. He said he could go. He didn't have to pay back anything.

Outside in the street this same foreman came across a man who owed him a few dollars. He called out to him. "Pay me—now!" "Please be patient. I will pay you back," the man answered. But the foreman wouldn't listen. He called the police. They arrested the man and put him in jail.

When the king heard about this he couldn't believe it. He sent for the foreman and had him put in prison.

The Lord forgives our sins and He expects us to forgive others. If we don't, He might just decide not to forgive us either.

Remember: We have to forgive other people.

August 19 Matthew 5

We should love our enemies

"Love your enemies. Pray for them!" (Matt. 5:44)

Some people say that we don't need to love and help everybody. If we don't like someone, we don't have to help him or her. We can treat him or her however we want to—it doesn't matter. Jesus says that's not true.

Jesus wants us to be nice to people we don't like. Even if they hurt us, we should still pray for them and ask the Lord to help them.

God gave us a good example of this. When He sends rain, does it rain only on the people He likes? No, it rains on all of us. It's the same with the sun. The sun doesn't shine only on some of us. The sun shines on both good and bad people.

So we can't pick and choose who we help, because it's wrong not to help others. God's children need to follow His example. We shouldn't treat anybody badly.

If someone really makes us very angry, do we still need to stay calm and friendly? Jesus says "yes." This is how His children should behave.

Remember: God's children shouldn't treat others badly.

Jesus tells His friends what makes Him happy

August 20 Luke 17

"Never talk others into doing something wrong." (Luke 17:1)

One day Jesus and His friends were talking together. Jesus told them how they should behave and answered their questions. What He said can help us.

- Sometimes we do things we shouldn't. It happens to everyone, but we should never talk others into doing something wrong. Be careful.
- If our brother or our friend does something wrong, tell them not to do it. If they say they're sorry, don't sulk and stay angry with them. It doesn't matter how often this happens. Every time he says he's sorry, we should forgive him.
- Jesus' friends asked Him to give them more faith. "Well," Jesus said, "with even a little bit of faith you can do great things. Just trust Me, I will help you."
- If someone works for you cleaning your house, would you go and clean her house all the time? No, because she works for you—you don't work for her. We work for the Lord—it's not the other way around. When He gives us something, all we can do is say thank you. We don't deserve it. And it's for free!

Remember: We should work for Jesus.

We can talk to the Lord

August 21 Matthew 6

"Pray like this." (Matt. 6:9)

Jesus taught us how to pray.

> "Our Father in heaven,
> May people see how important You are. There is no one like You.
> May You rule over all like a great king.
> Let the people on earth do Your will,
> just like all do in heaven.
> Please give us our food for today.
> Please forgive us for what we have done wrong,
> Just as we forgive others who hurt us.
> Please protect us against the Devil who wants us to sin.
> Help us not to listen to him and do wicked things.
> Amen."
>
> When we pray, we need to remember three things:
> - We should worship and praise God and ask that everyone will serve Him.
> - We can ask God to take care of us.
> - We need to ask God to forgive our sins.

Remember: We should pray regularly.

Don't pray if you don't mean what you say

August 22 Matthew 6

"Your father knows exactly what you need even before you ask Him!" (Matt. 6:8)

Often people just pray without thinking about what they're saying. The Lord says praying is like talking to Him. We can talk to Him about anything and everything, but we have to pray in the right way.

• It's wrong if we don't really care about talking to God but pray just so other people will be impressed. In Jesus' time people prayed at certain times of the day. Some people wanted others to hear how well they prayed. When prayer time came, they would go where lots of people were gathered. Then they prayed so that everybody could admire them. These people wanted to appear important, and they forgot that they were talking to God.

• It's wrong if people think that the longer they pray, the more the Lord will listen. If we want to have a long talk with the Lord, that's fine. He will be pleased. But we shouldn't think we're going to force the Lord into doing something just because of a long prayer. The Lord listens to us when we pray because He loves us, not because of the length of our prayers.

Remember: The Lord listens to us when we pray.

God listens when we pray

August 23 Matthew 7

"Keep on asking and you will be given what you ask for." (Matt. 7:7)

"**A**sk and I will give you what you ask for," the Lord said. "Keep on looking and you will find. Knock and I will open the door to you. Those who ask will receive." The Lord always listens to our prayers.

We need to remember that the Lord wants to give us only the best. To demonstrate this He said:

"A boy asks his dad for a slice of bread. Will his father give him a stone? Or if he asks for a fish, does he give him a snake? Of course not!" The Lord in heaven is much better than our fathers on earth. Where our earthly fathers give us good things, our heavenly Father gives us the best.

The Lord knows what is best for us.

Sometimes we ask for something and, when He doesn't give us what we asked for, we think God hasn't heard us. He has heard us, but it may be that what we asked for wasn't the right thing for us.

The Lord wants to give us something better. We have to trust Him.

Remember the Lord hears all our prayers. He answers them. He gives us what is best for us.

Remember: God knows best.

Do everything you can for God

August 24 Matthew 25

"Good work! Well done!" (Matt. 25:21)

One day a man had to go on a long journey so he gave each of his workers some money to do business for him while he was away. He gave one $5,000, a second $2,000, and the third one $1,000. Then he left to go on his trip.

The one who was given $5,000 began doing business right away and soon doubled the money. The worker who had $2,000 did the same, but the man who received $1,000 dug a hole in the ground and hid the money in it for safekeeping. After a long time the owner came back home. The workers with the $5,000 and $2,000 each gave him double his money back. He said, "Well done! You've done good work!" Next was the man with the $1,000. He gave the $1,000 back to the owner. He said, "Sir, I know you are a hard man so I hid the money. I was afraid I would lose it all." The owner was angry. "You lazy man," he said. "You could at least have put the money in a bank where it would have earned interest." The owner took the money from him and gave it to the other two men.

Like the money the man gave to his workers, God has given us talents. We must use them, not hide them.

Remember: We shouldn't hide the talents God has given us.

We need to give the Lord only the best

August 25 Luke 21

Jesus told them, "This poor woman has given more than all the rest." (Luke 21:3)

One day Jesus and His friends were at the temple. They watched as the people put their money onto the offering plate. There were lots of rich people. They put a lot of money on the plate. Then a poor widow came by. She dropped a few coins onto the offering plate.

It wasn't much, but Jesus said, "Do you know, this woman gave more than all the others? The other people put in a lot of money, but they could afford it, because they're rich. Even after giving a large sum, they have plenty of money left.

"This poor woman had only a few coins. She put all of them in the box. She has nothing left for food but she wanted to give the Lord the best she could, so she gave Him all she had."

The Lord sees into our hearts. He wants us to give Him our best. It doesn't matter if it isn't as much as other people give, as long as it comes from our hearts.

When we give to the Lord, it should be because we love Him and that will make Him very happy.

Remember: We should give to the Lord because we love Him.

Store up treasures in heaven

August 26 Matthew 6

"Store your treasures in heaven." (Matt. 6:20)

Some people want money so much that they work hard for it, but when they die their money means nothing to them. Their cars rust away. The moths eat their clothes and the food they stored up goes bad. They can't take anything with them.

Jesus says we shouldn't spend our time storing up money and possessions. We should spend our time making the Lord happy. "Store up treasures in heaven," He said. "Moths won't eat them there and they'll be safe from thieves.'

Long ago, a Christian leader, Augustine, was asked how to get treasures in heaven. He said that if you give something to everyone on their way to heaven, they can take it there for you. This is a way of getting treasures in heaven. If we give people smiles, we will get smiles back in heaven. If we help people, we will be helped in heaven. We could say that what we do for the Lord here on earth, He will do for us in heaven.

Remember: Spend time making the Lord happy.

Jesus will take care of you

August 27 John 10

"I am the good Shepherd." (John 10:11)

Jesus told a story to show how much He loved His friends. The story is about a shepherd and his sheep. He is a very good shepherd. He knows every one of his sheep. His sheep love him too. They want to be near him. In the morning when he comes into the sheep pen, they are happy. They want to go into the fields with him to graze. They know the shepherd will take them to the best places. We should be happy when we wake up, knowing that we can spend the day with Jesus. We should try to please Him.

Jesus went on with the story. One day a wolf tried to catch the sheep. Most shepherds would have left the sheep and run away, afraid that the wolf would attack them. The good shepherd doesn't do that. He fights the wolf, even though he knows the wolf can kill him. He will give his own life for his sheep. That's how much he loves them. And that's how much Jesus loves us. He gave His life on the cross for us. Someday our bodies will die, but God will bring us back to life again to live with Him in heaven forever.

Remember: God will take His children to heaven one day.

When you're afraid, He's there

August 28 Matthew 8

"Why are you afraid? Don't you have faith in Me?" (Matt. 8:26)

One day Jesus and His disciples started across the lake in a boat. Suddenly a terrible storm came up. A strong wind started blowing. The waves were so big that water swept over the sides into the boat.

Jesus was so tired that He was fast asleep. Jesus' friends were afraid. They thought the boat was going to sink. They woke Him up, shouting, "Lord, save us! We're going to drown."

Jesus said, "Why are you afraid? Don't you trust Me?"

Then He stood up. He told the waves and the wind to stop. Suddenly all was calm. Jesus' friends were amazed. The wind and the sea don't obey just anyone.

Jesus is with us now, just as He was in that boat with His friends. We might sometimes think that Jesus has forgotten about us—that's what His friends in the boat thought—but it's not true!

We shouldn't be afraid. Jesus is always with us. We can be sure of that.

Remember: We shouldn't be afraid because Jesus is with us.

You're never alone— Jesus is with you

August 29 John 5

"Stand up, pick up your mat and walk!" (John 5:8)

One day Jesus walked past the pool of Bethesda. Many sick people crowded around the pool. Some couldn't see and others couldn't walk. They believed that jumping into the water might make them well.

One of the men lying there had been sick for 38 years. Jesus asked the man, "Would you like to get well?" "I can't, Sir," the sick man said. "I have no one to help me into the pool."

Jesus said to him, "Stand up, pick up your mat, and walk!" Instantly the man was healed. He took his mat and walked away.

This happened on the Sabbath, a day set aside for praising God. The Pharisees saw what Jesus had done and were very angry. They said Jesus had broken the laws when He made the man well. They weren't even glad that Jesus had healed the man.

Jesus will be our friend even if we have no other friends. So we're never alone, because Jesus is with us.

Remember: Jesus' friends should never feel alone.

Jesus can do things for us that no one else can

August 30 John 11

"I will give you everlasting life." (John 11:25)

Lazarus, one of Jesus' friends, was sick. His sisters sent Jesus a message to come and help. Jesus didn't go right away. He waited for a few days. People didn't understand why, but Jesus had His reasons.

Four days later Jesus arrived at Lazarus' house. His sister, Martha, came running to Jesus, "Lord, if You had been here, my brother would not have died." Jesus answered, "Don't worry. I will bring him back to life again." Martha called her sister, Mary. Together they went to the grave. Jesus was sad when He saw everyone crying. The people were saying, "He loved Lazarus. If He had been here He might have helped him. Then Lazarus might not have died."

Then Jesus said, "Open up the grave." Martha tried to stop them. "Lord, he has been dead for four days!" Jesus' answer was, "Martha, didn't I tell you that you will see God's power?" So they opened up the grave. Jesus said, "Lazarus, come out!" And Lazarus came out of the grave. "Take him home," Jesus said.

Remember: Someday Jesus will raise the dead.

August 31 Luke 12

Be prepared and be faithful

"You will be glad if the Lord finds you busy working for Him." (Luke 12:43)

Jesus told another story. Once there was a man who had a large house. He had to go away for a while, so he asked one of his servants to take care of the place for him. He had to make sure that the other servants had what they needed.

What will the owner of the house do when he gets home and finds that the servant he left in charge has done everything he was asked to do? The owner will be very pleased. He will thank the man and treat him well.

But what if the owner comes back and finds that everything's a mess? The servant he left in charge said to himself, "The owner is taking too long to come back." So he started treating the other servants badly. He didn't do his work anymore and got drunk instead. The owner would not like this at all and would fire the man.

We need to be ready when the Lord comes again. That means we have to live every day in a way that pleases the Lord.

Remember: We have to be prepared for Jesus' second coming.

Serve the Lord now, before it's too late

September 1 Luke 16

"Listen to God's Word." (Luke 16:31)

One day there was a very rich man. A poor man named Lazarus sat at the rich man's back door. He found pieces of leftover food there. He was sick, but the rich man didn't help him.

Then Lazarus died. The angels carried him to heaven. The rich man also died, but he ended up in hell. He was doubled up with pain. Then in his misery he saw Lazarus and Abraham in the distance. He shouted, "Please help me. Send Lazarus with a drop of water. I am so thirsty in these flames."

Abraham answered, "During your life on earth you never helped anybody, including Lazarus. Now it's your turn to suffer."

The rich man pleaded, "Please send someone from heaven to warn my father and my five brothers, so that they don't end up in hell." Abraham said, "They have the Bible." The rich man replied, "But it will be better if someone talks to them from the dead." But Abraham said, "If they don't listen to the Bible, they won't listen to anything else."

The Bible tells us everything we need to know. We need to listen!

Remember: The Bible tells us everything we need to know.

September 2 Luke 15

The Lord loves us, faults and all

"When his father saw his son in the distance, he ran to him and put his arms around him." (Luke 15:20)

A father had two sons. The youngest said, "Dad, I want my share of your money now, instead of waiting until you die."

The boy's father gave him his share. The boy packed all his things and went on a journey to a faraway country. He went to one wild party after another there and wasted all his money. Eventually he didn't even have money for food. He got a job looking after pigs, but he was so hungry that he was tempted to eat the food the pigs ate.

Then he thought to himself, "There's enough food at home. I'll go back home to my father." So he went back home. He was still a long way from the house when his father saw him. He ran to his son and gave him a hug. The boy said, "I'm so sorry, Dad. I know I'm not good enough to be called your son anymore." His father didn't even listen, but told his servants, "Go and cook the best food. Bring the best clothes. My son was gone but now he's back."

The Lord is like this father. If we're sorry, He will forgive us.

Remember: God is our heavenly Father. He loves us very much.

We need to confess our sins

September 3 Luke 18

"O God, be merciful to me, for I am a sinner." (Luke 18:13)

One day Jesus told a story about two men who went to the temple to pray. One of them was an important man who seemed to be very religious. He didn't love God that much, but he wanted to make other people think he was better than they were. He prayed, "Lord, I want to thank you that I'm not a sinner like everyone else. I never cheat. I don't lie. I do everything I should." He went on and on about how great he was.

The other man was a tax collector. Everybody hated tax collectors. He knew he had made mistakes and he was ashamed of them. He didn't dare to lift his eyes to heaven as he prayed, "Oh God, I've done bad things. I'm a sinner. Please forgive me, even if I don't deserve it."

Which of these two prayers did the Lord like best? The second one, of course. The first man made the mistake of thinking that he was very important and that he didn't need God. The second man knew he needed the Lord because of all his sins. Only the Lord can forgive sins.

If we have done something wrong, we need to tell the Lord we are sorry, and mean what we say. Then we shouldn't do it again.

Remember: The Lord will forgive us our sins if we say we're sorry.

There are people who don't love Jesus

September 4 Matthew 21

"The farmer will give the farm to others." (Matt. 21:41)

Once a farmer had a beautiful farm with lots of fruit trees. He took good care of the trees. Then he had to go away for a long time. He decided to rent out his farm and the tenants agreed to give him a share of the fruit crop.

At harvest time he sent a worker to get his share of the fruit. The tenants refused to give it to him. They were rude to the worker, beat him up, and chased him off the farm. The owner tried again and sent another worker. The same thing happened to him. Next he sent his son. He thought they would be nice to his son. He was wrong—they killed him! They said, "If the boy is dead, there is no one to inherit the farm. Then we can keep it."

What will the owner do when he gets back? He will certainly punish those tenants severely.

God is like the owner who sent His Son to the people. Some of the people don't want to be His friend. One day, when God comes again, He will punish them.

Remember: People who don't listen to the Lord will be punished.

You find evil people everywhere

September 5 Matthew 13

"He planted weeds among the good seed." (Matt. 13:25)

There are people all over the world who don't like Jesus. Jesus told this story.

A farmer planted good seed in his field. One night, while everyone was asleep, people who didn't like him came to his field. They planted weeds among the good seed. Then they ran away.

The crop began to grow. The weeds looked a lot like the wheat. But one day the farmer's servant told him, "Sir, the field where you planted that good seed is full of weeds!" He realized that his enemies had planted the weeds.

"Shall we pull out the weeds?" the servants asked. "No," the farmer said, "you might pull out the wheat together with the weeds. Let them both grow together until the harvest. Then we'll be able to tell which is which. We'll burn the weeds and put the wheat in the barn."

This is the way it is in the world as well. People who love Jesus live among those who don't. When Jesus comes again, those who love Him will go to heaven with Him. The rest will be punished.

Remember: Those who don't love the Lord will be sorry.

To Jerusalem... Praise the Lord!

September 6 Matthew 21

"Praise Him who is coming. He is our Lord." (Matt. 21:9)

Jesus went to Jerusalem. The time for Him to be crucified was coming closer, and He knew it. He said to two of His friends, "Go to the village over there. You will see a donkey. Bring the donkey here. If anyone asks what you are doing, just say, 'The Lord needs him. He will send him back soon.'" So they brought Jesus the donkey. In the Old Testament it says that Jesus will ride into Jerusalem on a donkey. His friends threw clothes over the donkey's back. Then Jesus climbed onto the donkey and rode towards Jerusalem. Crowds gathered along the side of the road. Most of them spread their coats on the road ahead of Jesus. Others cut branches from palm trees and spread them across the road. This was their way of showing how great Jesus was. They treated Him like a king and shouted, "Praise the Lord. Bless the One who comes in the name of the Lord."

Everyone in Jerusalem came to see what was going on. "Who is this man?" they asked. And the crowds replied, "It's Jesus of Nazareth."

Jesus was crucified a few days later. But when He rose from the dead, He showed that He was indeed King of kings.

Remember: Jesus is more important than any ruler on earth.

A woman shows how important Jesus is

September 7 John 12

Jesus said, "Leave her alone. You will always have the poor among you." (John 12:7-8)

A little while before Jesus was crucified, Lazarus and his sisters Mary and Martha invited Him to dinner. Mary came up to Jesus with a small bottle of very expensive perfume. She rubbed the perfume on Jesus' feet. In those times it was a sign of great respect. Then Mary dried Jesus' feet with her long hair. The lovely smell filled the whole house.

But Judas Iscariot, who took care of the money, was very angry. He said, "Why waste the perfume like this? We could have sold it and given the money to the poor." Judas was the one who would soon betray Jesus. He didn't really want the money for the poor—he wanted it for himself.

Then Jesus said, "She only wanted to show how important I am to her. You will always have the poor among you. There will be enough time to help them. I am going away one of these days. Then it will be too late to do something for Me." We need to make the most of every chance we get to do things for the Lord.

Remember: Always try to do something to make Jesus happy.

Jesus celebrates Communion

September 8 Matthew 26

Jesus broke the bread and said, "Take it and eat it, for this is My body." (Matt. 26:26)

The night before Jesus was crucified He wanted to have supper with His friends one last time. "Where should we have the Passover supper?" His friends wanted to know. "Go to one of My friends in Jerusalem," Jesus said. "Ask him if we can eat the Passover meal at his house." The disciples did as Jesus told them.

As they were eating, Jesus took a loaf of bread and asked God's blessing on it. Then He broke it in pieces and gave each of His friends a piece, saying, "Take it and eat it. It is My body." Then He took a cup and gave thanks to God. He said, "Each of you drink from it. This is My blood poured out so that your sins can be forgiven. Then you will be friends of God again. You must celebrate this last supper until I come back. Every time you do it, remember Me." Then they sang a hymn and went to a garden called Gethsemane.

To this day we celebrate this last supper. We call it Communion. Every time we celebrate Communion, we remember that Jesus loves us and that He will come back to get us someday.

Remember: Someday, Jesus will come back to get us.

Judas the betrayer

September 9 Matthew 26

"The truth is, one of you will betray Me," Jesus said. (Matt. 26:21)

The leaders of the Jews didn't like Jesus. They wanted to kill Him. Judas went to them.

"I'll help you," he said. "How much will you pay me to betray Jesus?" They paid him 30 pieces of silver.

That night when Jesus and His friends had their last supper together, Judas was there.

Jesus knew what Judas was going to do. While they were eating, Jesus said, "One of you will betray Me." Jesus' friends were shocked.

Then Jesus said, "I will show you. It is the one who dips his bread in the dish with Me."

Judas pretended that he wasn't the one, but later that night he left. He told the soldiers that Jesus and His friends would be in the Garden of Gethsemane and that he would show them where to find Jesus.

It was terrible that one of Jesus' friends betrayed Him. It shows us that a person can sit in church and listen to the Devil instead of God. It breaks Jesus' heart.

Remember: Don't listen to the Devil. Listen to Jesus.

Jesus prays before He is captured

September 10 Matthew 26

"Don't do what I want. I want Your will, not Mine," Jesus said. (Matt. 26:39)

Jesus and His friends went to Gethsemane as they had planned. He asked His friends to wait for Him. He took three of His friends to pray with Him. One of them was Peter. "I'm afraid. Stay with Me. Could you stay awake and watch over Me?" Jesus said.

Jesus went on a little farther and prayed. "My Father! If it is possible, protect me. But don't do what I want. Do what You want." Then Jesus went back to His three friends. They were fast asleep. Jesus woke them up and said, "Couldn't you stay awake for Me even for a little while?" Then Jesus went back to pray. He said, "My Father, if I have to suffer, then let it be." When Jesus came back, His three friends were asleep again. He left them to sleep and went back to pray.

Finally He woke His friends and said, "Let's go. Judas, who will betray Me, is on his way."

Jesus died on the cross. He died for us. It was not easy for Him to do it, but He did it for us.

Remember: Jesus died on the cross for us.

Jesus is captured

September 11 Matthew 26

"He is the One I will greet with a kiss. Grab Him,'" Judas said. (Matt. 26:48)

After Jesus had prayed, Judas arrived. He brought a mob along with him who were armed with swords and clubs. They brought lights to look for Jesus. Judas identified Jesus. He said to the soldiers, "He is the One I will greet with a kiss. Grab Him." So he walked towards Jesus and greeted Him with a kiss. Then the soldiers arrested Jesus.

Peter pulled out his sword. He cut off the high priest's servant's ear. Jesus calmed him down. "Put away your sword," He said. "If you start killing people with your sword, you'll be killed yourself. I must be captured. If I don't want it to happen, I can ask the angels to help Me. Thousands of them are ready and waiting to do so. But this has to happen the way the Bible said it would, a long time ago."

Then Jesus turned to the soldiers and said, "Why are you armed with swords and clubs to arrest me? Am I some dangerous criminal? Why didn't you arrest Me when I taught in the temple? I was there every day."

Then the soldiers took Jesus away and the words of the prophets, recorded in the Bible a long time ago, came true.

Remember: A long time ago God prophesied that Jesus would die.

Jesus protects His friends

September 12 John 18

Jesus said, "Let my friends go." (John 18:8)

Just before the soldiers took Jesus away, something happened. All of Jesus' friends were in the Garden of Gethsemane with Him and the soldiers were going to arrest them too. But Jesus wouldn't let this happen.

Jesus asked the soldiers who they were looking for. They answered, "Jesus of Nazareth."

"I am Jesus of Nazareth," He said. "And since I am the one you want, let these others go."

Then Jesus' friends ran away. One of them was in such a hurry that he left some of his clothes behind!

All of Jesus' friends escaped. Some time before this Jesus had promised to protect them, and He kept His word. The soldiers just watched as Jesus' friends deserted Him. Although they were there to arrest Jesus, they couldn't do anything He didn't want.

Remember: Jesus will not desert His friends.

Peter denies Jesus

September 13 Matthew 26

Peter said, "I don't even know the man." (Matt. 26:72)

Peter and a friend of his followed the soldiers who had arrested Jesus. They wanted to see what would happen to Him. The soldiers took Jesus to the high priest's house. He was the most important of all the Jews and had to decide what to do with Jesus.

Peter sat outside in the courtyard. One of the high priest's servants said to him, "You were one of those with Jesus, weren't you?" But Peter denied it in front of everybody. "I don't know what you're talking about," he said.

Someone else noticed him and said, "Yes, he was with Jesus." Again Peter denied it, saying, "I don't know the man!" He even used bad language to show how serious he was. But then another man said, "I can tell by your accent that you're one of the men who hung around with Jesus." Now Peter shouted, "I swear I don't know this man!"

At that moment, Peter heard a rooster crow. Suddenly he remembered what Jesus had said to him at the Last Supper, "Before the rooster crows, you will say three times that you don't know Me."

Peter walked away crying bitterly.

Remember: Never be ashamed of being Jesus' friend.

Jesus is from God

September 14 Matthew 26

The high priest asked, "Are You Christ, the Son of God?" (Matt. 26:63)

The leader of the people was the high priest, Caiaphas. He called all the important leaders together. They were trying to find a reason to kill Jesus. People were saying bad things about Jesus, but they were lying. One said, "Jesus said He will destroy the temple." The high priest asked Jesus, "What do you say to this?" Jesus said nothing. Then the high priest asked Jesus, "Are You the One sent especially by God to come and help His people?" Jesus answered, "Yes, I am. It is true. You will see it is true."

The high priest called out, "You are insulting God! We don't need any more witnesses. You have shown us how wicked You are." Then the high priest pretended to be upset. He asked the others what he should do. "Guilty!" they shouted. "He must die!" Then they spat in Jesus' face and hit Him with their fists. "You are the Special One from God," they mocked Him. "Come on, tell us the names of those who are beating You up!"

Then they tied Jesus' hands and sent Him to Pilate, the Roman governor. He was the only one who could give the death sentence.

Remember: God sent Jesus to help us.

Jesus' trial before Pilate

September 15 Matthew 27

"Crucify Him!" they all shouted. (Matt. 27:22)

Jesus was brought before Pilate very early in the morning. "Are You the king of the Jews?" Pilate asked Him. "Yes," answered Jesus. Pilate talked to Jesus some more, but he couldn't find Jesus guilty of anything. He realized Jesus was innocent and he wanted to release Him. There was a murderer called Barabbas in jail. Pilate asked the crowd, "Which of these two do you want me to set free, Jesus or Barabbas?" The crowd shouted, "Barabbas!" Those who hated Jesus had stirred up the crowd to say this.

Pilate didn't know what to do. Even his wife had dreamed that Jesus was innocent. When the people wanted Barabbas freed, Pilate asked them, "What should I do with Jesus?" They shouted, "Crucify Him!" "Why?" asked Pilate. "What has He done?" But nobody was listening. They just yelled louder, "Crucify Him!" Pilate saw that nothing would make them change their minds so he washed his hands in a bowl of water and said, "You are the ones who want to kill Jesus. I am innocent of His death." The soldiers took Jesus away to crucify Him.

Remember: Jesus was not guilty, but He died for our sins.

Judas dies

September 16 Matthew 27

"I have done a terrible thing. Jesus was innocent and I betrayed Him." (Matt. 27:4)

Judas betrayed Jesus, but when he heard that Jesus was going to be crucified he felt very badly about what he had done. He took the money he'd been paid for betraying Jesus back to the high priest. He said, "I have done a terrible thing. Jesus was innocent and I betrayed Him." The priests answered, "That's your problem. Why should we care?"

Judas threw the money back at them. Then he went out and killed himself.

The priests at the temple wondered what to do with the money. They couldn't use it for the temple because it was payment for betrayal. They decided to buy a piece of land with the money. It would be used as a graveyard for people who didn't have any families.

We need to think before we act. We're often sorry about something we've done and sometimes it's too late to change it.

Remember: Think about what pleases God, before doing something wrong.

Jesus is crucified

September 17 Matthew 27

"T*his is Jesus, the King of the Jews.*" (Matt. 27:37)

The soldiers took Jesus away to crucify Him. But first they hurt Him very badly. They put a crown of long, sharp thorns on His head. They made fun of Him and spat in His face. They beat Him on the head with a stick. Then they gave Him His cross. He had to carry it Himself.

Jesus was crucified just outside the city. The place is called Golgotha, which means "Skull Hill". After a while Jesus couldn't carry the cross anymore so a man named Simon helped Him.

At Golgotha the soldiers nailed Jesus to the cross. They divided up His clothes among them and put a notice on the cross above Jesus' head. It said: "This is Jesus, the King of the Jews."

Two criminals were crucified with Jesus, one on either side of Him. One of them made fun of Jesus and mocked Him, but not the other one. Jesus told this man, "Today you will be with Me in paradise." The high priest and the other Jews also made fun of Jesus, "You saved others. So come down from the cross and save yourself." This is how Jesus suffered on the cross for each of us.

Remember: Jesus suffered on the cross for each one of us.

Jesus is the Son of God

September 18 Matthew 27

They said, "Truly, this was the Son of God." (Matt. 27:54)

Jesus was crucified at twelve o'clock, in the middle of the day. Suddenly it became dark and stayed that way until three o'clock. Then Jesus shouted out in a loud voice, "My God, My God, why have You left Me all alone?" The people standing near the cross couldn't make out exactly what He was saying, so they said, "Listen, He is calling the prophet Elijah to come and help Him." One of them put vinegar on a sponge for Jesus to drink. Then Jesus called out again, "I have done what I had to." His head fell forward and He died.

At that moment the earth shook. Rocks split apart. The curtain in the temple (that kept people out of the holy place of God) was torn in two. Even people who had died came back to life.

The soldiers who were guarding Jesus and the other two saw it all. They were terrified and said, "Truly, this was the Son of God."

Jesus' mother and some of her friends were there too. Jesus was dead—but it wasn't the end of the story.

Remember: Jesus did everything He could for us.

Jesus is buried

September 19 Matthew 27

Joseph took Jesus' body and buried it. (Matt. 27:59-60)

Late in the afternoon of the day Jesus was crucified, a rich man went to Pilate and asked for Jesus' body. He was one of Jesus' friends. His name was Joseph. He asked Pilate if he could bury the body. Pilate gave his permission.

So Joseph took Jesus' body and prepared to bury it. In those days they wrapped the bodies in a white cloth. They put all kinds of sweet-smelling herbs on the cloth. After doing this, Joseph put Jesus' body in a grave. The grave was like a room carved out of the rock. Joseph rolled a very big stone against the door of this room as he left.

Jesus' enemies went to Pilate the next day. They said, "Jesus said He would rise from the dead after three days. We think His friends are going to steal His body. Then they will say He has risen." So Pilate sent soldiers to guard the grave. If Jesus' disciples wanted to steal His body, they would stop them—but Jesus was only in the grave for three days.

Remember: When things seem really bad, wait to see what God can do.

September 20 Matthew 28

Jesus is raised from the dead

"Jesus isn't here anymore. He has been raised from the dead, just as He said." (Matt. 28:6)

At dawn on the Sunday morning after Jesus was crucified, Mary and Mary Magdalene went to see the grave.

Suddenly there was a great earthquake. An angel came down from heaven. He rolled away the stone at the opening of the tomb and sat on it. His face was shining like lightning. His clothes were white as snow. The guards shook with fear when they saw him. They were so frightened that they couldn't move. Some of them fainted.

Then the angel spoke to the women, "Don't be afraid. I know you're looking for Jesus. He isn't here anymore. He is alive again. He said it would happen. Come closer. This is where His body lay. See for yourselves, the grave is empty." Then the angel told the women to tell Jesus' friends what had happened.

As the women turned to go, they saw Jesus standing there. He spoke to them and said, "Don't be frightened. Go and tell My friends I am on my way to them."

The women hurried away to tell Jesus' friends.

Remember: Jesus' grave was empty. He rose from the dead.

Jesus' friends see Him

September 21 Luke 24

They were terribly frightened. They thought they were seeing a ghost. (Luke 24:37)

Jesus' friends talked about everything that had happened. There was the cross, then Jesus was buried, then the grave was empty, then Jesus appeared to the women. So many things had happened in just three days. While they were sitting there talking, something else happened. Suddenly Jesus was there with them. They were afraid. They thought they were seeing a ghost.

Jesus said to them, "Why are you afraid? Why do you doubt who I am? Look at My hands. Look at My feet. Touch Me and make sure I am not a ghost, because ghosts don't have bodies."

Jesus' friends were overjoyed. They couldn't believe their eyes. Jesus was really standing there with them. They could talk to Him again! Then Jesus asked them for something to eat. They gave Him a piece of fish and watched as He ate it. This was no ghost!

Then Jesus talked to them. He helped them to understand the Old Testament, which said that all these things would happen. The promises that God had made then had come true.

Remember: Jesus made it clear—God keeps His promises.

September 22 Luke 24

Jesus appears to two men

"The Lord has really risen! He appeared to Peter!" (Luke 24:34)

Two of Jesus' friends were on their way to Emmaus, a village near Jerusalem. As they walked along, Jesus started walking beside them. They didn't recognize Him. Jesus asked them, "What are you talking about?" One of the men, Cleopas, replied, "You must be the only person in Jerusalem who hasn't heard about all the things that have happened the last few days." "What things?" Jesus asked.

"The things that happened to Jesus, the man from Nazareth. He preached beautifully. He also did amazing things. Then the chief priests and rulers arrested Him and He was crucified. We really hoped He was going to help us."

Jesus said, "Don't you believe what the Old Testament says? All of these things had to happen to Jesus." Then Jesus explained to them how God had made all His promises in the Old Testament come true.

It was getting late. While they were having supper together, they suddenly recognized Jesus. They were very excited and they hurried to tell everybody that Jesus really was alive again.

Remember: People hoped that Jesus would help them and He did.

Thomas exclaims, "My Lord and my God"

September 23 John 20

Thomas said to Jesus, "My Lord and my God." (John 20:28)

One night all of Jesus' friends were together, including Thomas, who hadn't been with them when they first saw Jesus. They had told Thomas about it but he didn't believe them. How can a dead person come back to life?

That night all the doors were locked. Yet, suddenly, Jesus was there with them. He said, "Peace be with you." He looked at Thomas and said, "Put your finger here and see My hands. Touch them. Come, put your hand here where they put the sword in." Jesus wanted Thomas to know that He had really come back to life.

Thomas had seen Jesus nailed to the cross. Now He was standing in front of him, alive. How was it possible? Only God could have done it. All that Thomas could say was, "My Lord and my God."

Jesus said to him, "You believe because you have seen Me. There will be people who will not see Me with their eyes. They will also believe and they will be happy." We can't see Jesus with our eyes but we know He is there and it makes us happy.

Remember: We cannot see Jesus but we know He is here.

September 24 John 21

Jesus appears to His friends again

Then one of Jesus' friends said to Peter, "It is the Lord!" (John 21:7)

"**I**'m going fishing," Peter said. "We'll come too," his friends said, so they went out on the lake in their boat. They caught nothing all night.

At sunrise, they saw someone standing on the beach, but they couldn't see who it was. He called out, "Have you caught any fish?" "No," they replied. "Throw out your net on the other side of the boat, and you'll get plenty of fish!"

They did, and they caught so many fish that the net was too heavy to pull into the boat.

One of Jesus' friends then said to Peter, "That man is the Lord." Peter jumped into the water right away and started swimming. They weren't far from the shore. The others followed in the boat. When they got there, Jesus already had a fire burning and was busy cooking fish over it. There was bread as well, and His friends brought some of the fish they'd just caught. They had a nice meal together.

Jesus' friends knew He was alive. He had died, but now He was alive again. It made them so happy.

Remember: The Lord lives!

Jesus wants us to love Him

September 25 John 21

"Simon, do you love Me?" Jesus asked. (John 21:15)

Jesus and Peter were talking after breakfast.

Jesus asked Peter, "Peter, do you love Me?"

Peter answered Jesus, "Yes, Lord, You know I love You." Jesus said, "Then you must take good care of God's children."

Jesus asked him a second time, "Peter, do you love Me?" "Of course, Lord, You know that I love You," Peter answered. "Look after my people," Jesus said.

Jesus asked Peter a third time, "Do you love Me?" This made Peter very sad. "Lord, You know everything. You know I love You." And again Jesus said, "Take good care of the children of God."

Then Jesus went away. But He made sure His friends weren't alone. They had to be one another's friends.

Christians need to take care of each other. It pleases the Lord.

Remember: Christians should help each other.

Jesus sends His people to tell everybody about Him

September 26 Matthew 28

"Go to all people. Tell them about Me and make them My friends." (Matt. 28:19)

Before Jesus went back to heaven, He told His friends what He wanted them to do.

He said, "No one is as powerful as I am. I am the most powerful of all in heaven and on earth. Go tell all people everywhere about Me. Make them My friends."

"If they believe in Me, baptize them. Then tell them how to be good Christians. Tell them what makes God happy."

Jesus went on talking. He told them, "You are almost like people who have the keys to heaven. When you tell someone about Me, you unlock heaven's door to him or her. If someone won't listen, you can lock him or her out of heaven. And always remember—I am with you. I will always be with you."

If we are Jesus' friends, we need to tell our friends about Him. Just think how happy Jesus will be if we and all our friends love Him.

Remember: We need to tell our friends that Jesus wants to be their friend.

Jesus sends us a special Helper

September 27 John 16

"When the Holy Spirit comes, He will help you to do and think what is right." (John 16:13)

We have heard all about the things Jesus did. Next we hear what happened to His friends after Jesus went to heaven.

Jesus said His friends should tell everybody about Him. We need to do the same if we are His children. Sometimes we feel a little nervous about doing this, but Jesus said we should never be afraid. He sends us a special Helper. This is the Holy Spirit. The Holy Spirit is very powerful. The Spirit knows what God wants. That's how He knows how to help us.

We shouldn't be afraid of the Devil. The Holy Spirit is there to help us and to protect us.

If we don't know what to do, we can pray. The Holy Spirit will tell us what to do. We need to pray to God every day and ask Him to help us. Remember, we have a special Helper—the Holy Spirit.

We can't see the Holy Spirit, but that doesn't mean He isn't there. The Spirit is in us and that's why He can really help us.

Remember: God sent the Holy Spirit to be our special Helper.

Jesus is going to get our place in heaven ready

September 28 John 14

"Trust God, and trust in Me." (John 14:1)

When Jesus was still with His friends on earth, He told them that one day He would go back to heaven, where His Father is. His friends didn't really understand what He meant, so Jesus told them why He was going there.

Imagine that a father's children have been away from home for a very long time, but the father knows they are coming home the next day. What does he do? Of course he will make sure that their beds are made, their rooms are neat, and that there's enough to eat. Everything must be just right.

Jesus says that He will do the same for us. He is going back to His Father's house to get everything ready. All God's children are going to heaven one day. Jesus will make sure that our place is ready for us. If we are God's children, there is room for us to live with Jesus in heaven, the home of God.

We should be happy that Jesus went to heaven, and we can be sure our place in heaven is ready.

Remember: Jesus has prepared a special place for us in heaven.

Five girls are ready and five are not

September 29 Matthew 25

"Be ready. You don't know when the Lord is coming." (Matt. 25:13)

We always have to give the Lord only our best. If He comes today, we want Him to be happy with us. Listen to this story.

In the olden days they did things differently at weddings. First the men had a party at the groom's house. The women dressed the bride at her home. When the men were ready, they walked from the groom's house to the bride's house. The guests waited along the road. When the men came past, they joined them. Everybody had lamps, which they carried as they walked together to the bride's house.

Once there were ten girls waiting like this for the bridegroom. He took a long time. The lamps of five of the girls went out. They wanted to borrow oil for their lamps from the other girls, but the others only had enough for themselves. So they had to go get oil. While they were away, the bridegroom came past. The girls who were waiting for him along the road joined him, and together they went to the wedding. The other five arrived at the wedding too late. They were locked out.

We have to be ready when the Lord comes for us.

Remember: Be sure to be ready if the Lord comes today.

The disciples wait for the Holy Spirit in Jerusalem

September 30 Acts 1

One day when Jesus and His disciples were having a meal, Jesus told them, "Do not leave Jerusalem until my Father sends you the heavenly Present He promised you." (Acts 1:4)

After rising from the dead, Jesus appeared to His disciples from time to time. He talked to them often. Once, while they were all having a meal together, Jesus told the disciples they should stay on in Jerusalem after He left them. God was going to send His Holy Spirit to come upon them.

The Spirit would give them power to do God's work on earth. From that time on believers would be witnesses for Jesus. They would tell people about Jesus in Jerusalem and everywhere—even to the ends of the earth. The Spirit would take away their shyness and help them say openly that Jesus was their Savior.

Not long after He said this, Jesus was taken up into the sky. Jesus' friends stood watching as He disappeared into a cloud. As they stood there, amazed, two angels in white clothes suddenly appeared among them. They said, "Jesus has been taken away from you into heaven. He is now ruling in heaven as Lord of the whole world. And someday, just as you saw Him go, He will return!"

Remember: Jesus is not gone. He is with us always.

A new disciple is chosen

October 1 Acts 1

Peter said, "So now we need to choose someone else to take Judas' place. It must be someone who has been with us all the time that we were with the Lord Jesus—from the time He was baptized by John until the day He was taken from us to heaven." (Acts 1:21-22)

After Jesus went to heaven, the apostles and other believers gathered together in the upstairs room of the house where they were staying in Jerusalem. There were about 120 believers together in the room that day. Among them were Jesus' brothers and some women.

Then Peter stood up and told them that Judas, who had betrayed Jesus, had died.

There had to be twelve apostles, so Peter said they should choose a new one to take Judas' place. It had to be someone who had been with them all the time they followed Jesus, someone who saw everything Jesus did.

They thought of two men—Barsabbas and Matthias—and they prayed for the right man to be chosen. The Lord then helped them and they chose Matthias.

Remember: We should pray to God and listen to Him when we have to make decisions.

The Holy Spirit comes

October 2 Acts 2

Then, what looked like flames or tongues of fire appeared and settled on each of them. And everyone was filled with the Holy Spirit and began speaking in other languages. It was the Holy Spirit who helped them. (Acts 2:3-4)

On the day of Pentecost, an important feast that the Jews celebrated every year, the believers were gathered together in Jerusalem.

Suddenly, there was a sound from heaven like the roaring of a mighty wind. Then something like flames came down and settled on Jesus' friends. It was the Holy Spirit. He had come to fill all the believers with His power. The believers found they could speak in other languages.

Lots of people in Jerusalem heard this mighty sound and came running to see what was happening. During Pentecost, people from many nations came to Jerusalem. They spoke many different languages. "How can this be?" they exclaimed. "All of us can hear these people speaking in our own languages about the wonderful things God has done."

The day that the Holy Spirit came to the believers was the beginning of a new time for them. The Spirit now stays in each of us. He helps us with the way we live, so people can see we love Jesus.

Remember: The Holy Spirit makes us children of God.

Peter preaches on Pentecost

October 3 Acts 2

Peter told the crowd, "What you see this morning was predicted centuries ago by the prophet Joel: 'In the last days,' God said, 'I will pour out my Spirit upon all people.'" (Acts 2:16-17)

The crowd stood listening to the believers with amazement. "What can this mean?" they asked each other. Others said, "They're drunk, that's all!" Peter stepped forward: "It isn't true!" he said, and then he explained to them what was happening. The prophet Joel had written in the Old Testament that God would send His Spirit to His children on earth. Old and young, men and women—everybody would be filled with the Holy Spirit.

Joel's words came true on the day of Pentecost. Since that day every Christian shares in the power of the Holy Spirit—including us. We should never think we're too young or not important enough. The Holy Spirit will not forget us. He lives in us and makes us part of the Lord's church. He is the one who helps us love God and other people. He stops us when we want to say or think bad things. The Spirit guides us every day to do what God tells us. All we need to do is to allow the Spirit into our lives and let Him help us with the way we live, so God can be proud of us.

Remember: The Holy Spirit is with us every day.

A new church in Jerusalem

October 4 Acts 2

Those who believed what Peter said were baptized and added to the church. (Acts 2:41)

After Peter preached at Pentecost, the lives of many people changed. Almost three thousand of them started believing in the Lord Jesus that day. They became part of the church in Jerusalem, and what a wonderful church it was! Everybody loved the Lord.

The new believers came to listen to Peter and the other apostles every day. Once a week was not good enough for them. They wanted to learn all about Jesus. They wanted to know exactly what He had done to make them His children.

The Christians cared for each other and shared everything they had. If anyone was having a problem, there was always someone to help. They were like brothers and sisters. They prayed together and had their meals together. Everybody in Jerusalem could tell they believed in Jesus.

When we care for each other as Christians, people notice. It makes them want to join the church. But if we're always fighting and making trouble, nobody's going to feel like following Jesus. We need to live so that others want to hear more and more about Jesus.

Remember: The Holy Spirit helps us to love other people.

Believers care for each other

October 5 Acts 4

All the believers loved one another, and they shared everything they had. (Acts 4:32)

It must have been wonderful to belong to the first church in Jerusalem. They truly loved the Lord and cared for each other. If any Christians were hungry, the others would sell their land or houses and bring the money to the apostles to give those in need.

Barnabas, for example, was a member of the church. He sold a field he owned and brought the money to the apostles. God used this money to take care of them so that no member of the church went to bed on an empty stomach. There was more than enough for everybody to live on.

If we are the Lord's children we shouldn't keep our money just for ourselves. We should share it with friends who don't have enough food or warm clothes. We need to know right from the start that our money belongs to the Lord and we should give part of it back to Him.

If we are selfish and only want more and more money, toys, and clothes, we make God upset. Our lives belong to Him.

Remember: Our money belongs to the Lord.

Peter heals a lame man

October 6 Acts 3

Peter said to the lame man, "I don't have any money for you. But I'll give you what I have. In the name of Jesus Christ of Nazareth, get up and walk!" (Acts 3:6)

Peter and John went to the temple one afternoon to pray. Just outside the temple, at the gate, they saw a lame man. This man had never walked from the day he was born. His family put him beside the gate each day, so that he could beg for money.

When Peter and John walked past him, he asked them for money. Peter didn't have any money with him. But he had something far better for the lame man. Peter looked him in the eyes. Then he told the man to get up and walk.

Right there, in front of everybody, Peter took the lame man by the hand and helped him up. And all at once, his legs were healed. He was so happy that he started jumping up and down. Then he walked into the temple with Peter and John praising the Lord. He knew it was God who had healed him.

All the people saw him walking and heard him praising the Lord. They recognized him immediately. They couldn't believe this was the same man. God performed a great miracle that day.

Remember: God still heals sick people today.

Peter and John before the council

October 7 Acts 4

The Council called the apostles back in and told them never again to speak or teach about Jesus. But Peter and John replied, "Do you think God wants us to obey you rather than Him? We cannot stop telling about the wonderful things we have seen and heard." (Acts 4:18-20)

After Peter had healed the lame man in the name of Jesus, many people came to him in the temple. He started telling them about Jesus. He also told them to stop sinning and to believe in Jesus.

The rulers and elders in the temple were very upset with Peter. They had him and John arrested. The next day the temple guards brought the two apostles before the council of all the leaders and elders of the nation. They told Peter and John to stop telling people about Jesus. They refused. They said they were never going to stop talking about Jesus.

The council members were angry. But they were also worried, because so many people had seen the man healed. They let the apostles go.

Jesus still performs miracles today. We should never be ashamed to say we are His children. Even if others make fun of us, it doesn't matter because Jesus is the most important Person in the whole world.

Remember: We shouldn't be ashamed to speak about the Lord.

October 8 Acts 5

Ananias and Sapphira tell a lie

Then Peter said, "Ananias, why has Satan made you lie? Why did you keep some of the money for yourself? You pretended to give everything to the church." (Acts 5:3)

Ananias and his wife, Sapphira, belonged to the church in Jerusalem. They were dishonest. They sold some property but Ananias only gave part of the money to Peter. He kept some for himself, but he told Peter that he had given him every penny. This was a lie.

Peter was sad that Ananias had lied. He said, "The property was yours to sell or not to sell, as you wished. The money was yours, and you could do whatever you wanted with it. So why did you lie to God?" As soon as Ananias heard these words he fell down dead.

A little while later his wife came in. She didn't know what had happened. She also lied to Peter and the same thing happened to her. She fell to the floor and died.

The Lord doesn't like it when we lie. We need to tell the truth, even if it isn't always easy. Sometimes we are tempted to lie to get out of trouble but we should always tell the truth.

Remember: God's children always tell the truth.

Peter and his friends are freed from prison

October 9 Acts 5

The Council arrested the apostles and put them in jail. But an angel of the Lord came at night, opened the gates of the jail, and brought them out. (Acts 5:18-19)

The apostles performed lots of miracles and wonders among the people. Their prayers were healing the sick. More and more people believed and joined the church in Jerusalem. This made the high priest and his friends very jealous. They arrested the apostles and put them in jail.

That night the Lord sent an angel to open the doors of the prison and bring the apostles out. The next morning they were back at the temple.

When the council heard about this they sent soldiers to go and arrest the apostles. "Didn't we tell you never again to teach in this Man's name?" the high priest demanded. Peter and the apostles told them they would not stop. The council was furious! But instead of killing the apostles, they had them whipped and then let them go.

Not one of the apostles was embarrassed about believing in Jesus. And they didn't complain about being beaten for talking about Jesus.

Remember: Talk often to others about Jesus.

Stephen is killed

October 10 Acts 7

Then Stephen fell to his knees, shouting, "Lord, don't charge them with this sin!" (Acts 7:60)

The apostles realized that they couldn't do all the work in the church anymore, so they chose seven men to take care of the poor. One of them was Stephen. Some who weren't part of the church got very angry with him because he said God didn't live in the temple.

These men told lies about Stephen. They said they'd heard him speaking against the temple and mocking Moses. Everyone in the council was very angry.

Stephen was arrested and brought before the council. He explained what he believed to the council and the high priest. In his speech he said that the Jewish leaders were responsible for killing Jesus. This made them furious.

At that moment Stephen could see into heaven. He saw Jesus standing at God's right hand. He told the Jewish leaders this. They were horrified and decided to kill him. They dragged Stephen out of the city and stoned him to death.

As Stephen lay dying he prayed for his killers. He asked the Lord to forgive them. We too should also pray for people who don't like us.

Remember: Don't speak badly of others.

Simon the magician

October 11 Acts 8

The believers who had fled Jerusalem went everywhere preaching the Good News about Jesus. Philip, for example, went to the city of Samaria and told the people there about Christ. (Acts 8:4-5)

After Stephen was killed, the Jewish leaders started throwing Christians in Jerusalem into jail. Many fled. A Christian called Philip went to the city of Samaria, where he told the people about Jesus.

There was a well-known sorcerer (magician) called Simon who lived in Samaria. When Simon saw how people were starting to believe in Jesus and were being baptized, he decided to be baptized himself.

Some time later Peter and John visited the city. They prayed for these new Christians and the Holy Spirit came upon them. When Simon saw this happen, he offered Peter money to buy this power of the Holy Spirit. Peter was very angry with him. He told Simon to stop his evil ways immediately and pray to the Lord or he'd be punished.

No one can buy the power of the Lord. His power only works for people whose hearts belong to Him. If we listen to the Lord then His Spirit will work in us.

Remember: Only those who believe in Jesus are children of God.

Philip and the Ethiopian

October 12 Acts 8

A very important man from Ethiopia was on his way back home. Sitting in his carriage, he was reading aloud from the book of the prophet Isaiah. The Holy Spirit said to Philip, "Go over and walk along beside the carriage." (Acts 8:28-29)

One day the Lord spoke to Philip. He told him to walk along a quiet road leading from Jerusalem to Gaza. As he did so a carriage passed by. Sitting in the carriage was a very important man from Africa. He was the head of the household of the queen of Ethiopia. This man was reading from the book of Isaiah.

The Holy Spirit told Philip to walk over to the carriage and speak to the man. Philip asked him, "Do you understand what you're reading?" The man asked how he could understand it when there was no one to explain it to him. So Philip explained what was written in the Bible and told the Ethiopian about Jesus.

The Ethiopian was so happy to hear the good news about Jesus that he asked Philip to baptize him. Afterwards Philip went on his way and, with great joy in his heart, the Ethiopian went back home to Africa.

Remember: The Bible is the Word of God.

Saul's conversion

October 13 Acts 9

Saul fell to the ground and heard a voice saying to him, "Saul! Saul! Why are you persecuting Me?" "Who are you, Sir?" Saul asked. And the voice replied, "I am Jesus, the One you are persecuting!" (Acts 9:4-5)

A man called Saul lived in Jerusalem. We also know him as Paul. At first he hated the Christians and he was very glad when Stephen was killed. He wanted all the Christians to be wiped out.

When Saul heard that there were lots of Christians living in the city of Damascus, he asked the high priest for a letter giving him permission to arrest the believers there. Then he set off for Damascus.

On the way there, a brilliant light from heaven suddenly beamed down on him. Saul was frightened and fell to the ground. Then Jesus spoke to Saul. He asked him why he was trying to destroy His followers. When Saul got up he couldn't see anything. He was blind. The people with him had to take his hand and lead him to Damascus.

There was a believer in Damascus called Ananias. The Lord sent him to pray for Saul in the house where Saul was staying. After Ananias had prayed, Saul could see again and he was filled with the Holy Spirit.

Remember: Nobody is too evil for God to save.

Peter brings Tabitha back to life

October 14 Acts 9

But Peter asked them all to leave the room; then he knelt and prayed. Turning to the body he said, "Get up, Tabitha." (Acts 9:40)

Peter traveled from place to place visiting believers. One day he arrived in Lydda. He healed a man there called Aeneas who had been paralyzed for a long time.

A believer called Tabitha lived in Joppa, a town nearby. She got sick and died. Her friends asked Peter to come right away. As soon as he arrived they took him to her room. Everybody was very sad and some were crying. Peter asked them all to leave the room. He knelt down by Tabitha's bed and prayed. Then he turned to the body and told her to get up.

Tabitha opened her eyes. She was alive. It was a miracle! The news spread through the town. Many people started believing in Jesus.

Jesus can raise people from the dead. One day He will bring us back to life again and we will live in heaven with Him forever. Jesus is stronger than death. Jesus overcame death when He came back to life on the third day so we never have to be afraid of death.

Remember: Jesus is stronger than death.

Cornelius' vision

October 15 Acts 10

In Caesarea there lived a Roman army officer named Cornelius. He helped the poor and was a man who regularly prayed to God. (Acts 10:1-2)

Cornelius was an important Roman soldier. He was captain of the Italian Regiment. He prayed to God a lot. One afternoon at about three o'clock he was praying when suddenly he saw an angel of God coming towards him.

"Cornelius!" the angel said. "The Lord has noticed your prayers and gifts to the poor!" The angel told him to send some men down to Joppa to get Peter.

The next day Peter went up onto the flat roof of the house where he was staying. It was about twelve o'clock, and as he was praying there he saw something like a sheet coming down from the sky. In the sheet were all sorts of animals that the Jews weren't allowed to eat. Then a voice told him to eat them. "Never, Lord," Peter said. The same thing happened three times.

While Peter was still wondering what the vision meant, three men sent by Cornelius came looking for him. They told Peter that Cornelius wanted him to go to his house. So the next day he left for Caesarea with the three men.

Remember: It helps to pray. God listens.

Cornelius' whole life changes

October 16 Acts 10

Even as Peter was saying these things, the Holy Spirit fell upon all who had heard the message. (Acts 10:44)

When Peter arrived in Caesarea he went straight to Cornelius' house. Cornelius, his relatives, and close friends were waiting for him and invited Peter in.

Peter told him that according to Jewish law he wasn't allowed to enter the home of a non-Jew but, since the Lord had sent him there, he would go in.

Cornelius told Peter about the angel who instructed him to send for Peter. At last Peter understood the meaning of the vision of the sheet. It was the Lord showing him not to think of anyone as unclean. He realized that nobody is so bad or sinful that he can't hear God's word.

Peter told everybody gathered together in Cornelius' house about Jesus. As he was talking, the Holy Spirit fell on all who heard the message. Peter was happy to see that God also gave His Spirit to those who weren't Jews. Cornelius and the others were baptized.

We should never think that we're better than others. The Lord loves all of us the same. He has no favorites.

Remember: The Lord cares about everybody.

Peter in trouble with the church in Jerusalem

October 17 Acts 11

When Peter arrived back in Jerusalem, some of the Jewish believers criticized him. "You went into the home of non-Jews and even ate with them!" they said. (Acts 11:2-3)

The news of the conversion of Cornelius spread quickly. Some of the believers in Jerusalem were very angry when they heard about it. They were Jews and they felt it was wrong of Peter to enter the house of a heathen.

When Peter arrived back in Jerusalem, they told him he shouldn't have gone into Cornelius' house. He certainly shouldn't have eaten with him. But Peter told them exactly how it came about and they were satisfied with his explanation.

Some people think they're better than others who speak a different language or who have a different skin color. This is a sin in the eyes of the Lord. Some Jewish believers thought they were too good to go into the homes of heathens and talk to them about Jesus. God showed them they were wrong and they listened to Him. We need to tell everybody about Jesus.

Remember: All people are equally important to the Lord.

Paul works in Antioch

October 18 Acts 11

Then Barnabas went on to Tarsus to find Paul. When he found him, he brought him back to Antioch. Both of them stayed there with the church for a full year, teaching many people. (Acts 11:25-26)

Many of the believers who had fled from Jerusalem earlier were living in Antioch. They began preaching about Jesus to the people of that city and soon the church there had many members. Jews, as well as other people who spoke Greek, started believing in Jesus.

When the apostles heard how well the church in Antioch was doing, they sent Barnabas to help them. Barnabas was a good man, full of the Holy Spirit. He taught the believers to do everything the Lord said.

Eventually Barnabas couldn't do all the work of the church on his own anymore so he decided to send for Paul to help him.

During this time someone brought bad news to the Christians in Antioch. The people of the church in Jerusalem were suffering because of a great famine. The believers in Antioch started collecting money right away, and Paul and Barnabas took it to the elders of the church in Jerusalem.

Remember: We should share our money with those in need.

An angel helps Peter escape from prison

October 19 Acts 12

Suddenly, there was a bright light in the cell, and an angel of the Lord stood before Peter. The angel tapped him on the side to wake him up and said, "Quick! Get up!" And the chains fell off his wrists. (Acts 12:7)

King Herod Agrippa did not like the Christians in Jerusalem at all. He had an apostle called James killed, which pleased the Jewish leaders. Then Herod arrested Peter and sent him to jail. Peter was chained between two soldiers while two others guarded the prison gate.

That night when Peter was asleep, with a soldier on either side, an angel suddenly stood before him. The chains fell from his wrists. Then the angel led the way out of the cell. Peter thought he was dreaming. It was only when he was standing outside in the street that he realized what had happened. "It's really true!" he said to himself.

He went to the home of Mary, John Mark's mother, where many believers had gathered to pray. They didn't believe the servant girl when she came running inside crying, "Peter is standing at the door!" "You're crazy," they said, but in the end they opened the door and were overjoyed to see Peter standing there.

Remember: No problem is ever too big for the Lord to solve.

Paul and Barnabas' first missionary journey

October 20 Acts 13

One day believers were worshipping the Lord and fasting in Antioch. Then the Holy Spirit said to them, "I have special work for Barnabas and Paul. Send them out now to do it." (Acts 13:2)

One day the believers in Antioch were praying together and fasting when the Holy Spirit showed them that they should send Paul and Barnabas to go and do missionary work.

Paul and Barnabas sailed for the island of Cyprus. They preached from town to town until they finally reached Paphos. There they met a Jewish sorcerer called Elymus. He was with Sergius Paulus, the governor of the island.

The governor had heard about Paul and Barnabas. He invited them to visit him because he wanted to hear them preach. Elymus tried to put a stop to this. Paul turned on him and said God would punish him for trying to stop them. Elymus would be blind for a time. Elymus lost his sight immediately. After this, the governor believed in the Lord.

The Lord does not allow anything to stand in His way. If He wants to save someone, He will do it. We should never think we can run away from Him. The best thing we can ever do is to give our lives to Him.

Remember: Every Christian is a witness for the Lord.

Paul heals a lame man

October 21 Acts 14

At Lystra there was a man with crippled feet. He had been that way from birth, so he had never walked. So Paul called to him in a loud voice, "Stand up!" (Acts 14:8-10)

Paul and Barnabas preached in a city called Iconium. A lot of Jews and Gentiles started believing. This made the Jewish leaders angry and they starting causing trouble for the apostles. Eventually Paul and Barnabas had to run for their lives. They moved on to Lystra.

In Lystra, Paul preached again. Among the people listening to him was a man who had been lame from birth. Paul told him to get up and walk. Instantly the man did just that!

When the crowd saw this they thought Paul and Barnabas were gods. This really upset the two apostles. "Why do you think such a thing?" they cried. "We work for Jesus. He is the one who performs the miracles."

Some troublesome Jews stirred up the crowds and told them to kill Paul. They stoned Paul, dragged him out of the city, and left him there for dead. But God saved Paul's life.

Remember: Jesus cares about people's needs.

October 22 Romans 3

Paul talks about God's goodness

All have sinned. All are far away from God. Yet now God in His kindness declares us not guilty. He has done this through Christ Jesus, who has freed us by taking away our sins. (Rom. 3:23-24)

Paul preached to lots of people in lots of different places. He also wrote quite a few letters to different churches. In his letter to the Romans Paul talks about how much God is willing to do so we can become His children. Paul says we are all sinners. Not one of us can become the Lord's child on our own. Even if we try our best to live the way we should and to obey God's laws, we just cannot help sinning.

God thought of a way to save us. He sent Jesus to us and Jesus took all our sins onto His shoulders. He died on the cross in our place.

If we believe in Jesus, our sins don't count anymore. He has already punished Jesus for our sins. We don't need to give God money to save ourselves. It doesn't do any good to tell Him how good we are. Neither will help us. There is only one way that works. We have to tell God that we're sorry for all our sins and ask Jesus if we can put our sins onto His shoulders. God will forgive us and we will become His children.

Remember: Jesus died for our sins.

God sent Jesus to die in our place

October 23 2 Corinthians 5

God made Christ, who never sinned, to be the offering for our sin. If we belong to Jesus, our sins don't count to God anymore. Then we are free! (2 Cor. 5:21)

Paul couldn't stop writing about everything God does to save us. He tells the Christians in Corinth that Jesus never does anything bad. He isn't a sinner like we are. But He loves us so much that He was willing to leave His heavenly home and become a human being. Jesus took all our sins on Himself there on the cross—every single one. He paid even for our sins that are still to come!

When God looked at Jesus on the cross He saw only our sins. He punished Jesus with death instead of us. We actually should have been the ones hanging there. We should have taken our own punishment. But Jesus did it in our place. He died so that God would not punish us.

God loves us so much that He was prepared to let His Son die for us. God doesn't want even one of us to be lost. Believe in Jesus and know that He paid for all your sins with His blood.

Remember: God is not angry with us any more.

The meeting of the apostles in Jerusalem

October 24 Acts 15

When they arrived in Jerusalem, Paul and Barnabas were welcomed by the whole church, also the apostles and elders. They told them all that God had done through them. But then some stood up and said, "All new Christians must obey the law of Moses." (Acts 15: 4-5)

Paul and Barnabas told all the people they met about Jesus. Some Jewish believers then said that these new Christians had to become just like them. Paul didn't agree. Then the church in Antioch sent Paul and Barnabas to Jerusalem to talk about this disagreement.

The apostles welcomed Paul and Barnabas to Jerusalem. There were a few believers who didn't agree with Paul. They wanted all Christians to obey Jewish laws. So the leaders of the church held a meeting to decide on the right thing to do. Peter said he didn't think it was necessary for everybody to obey Jewish laws. James, Jesus' brother, felt the same way. Most agreed with them.

So the church leaders wrote a letter to send to all the churches. In the letter they explained what they had decided at their meeting. Paul and Barnabas were happy, because now they could carry on teaching the non-Jews about Jesus.

Remember: God accepts all who believe in Jesus.

A jailer tries to kill himself

October 25 Acts 16

The chief jailer asked Paul and Silas, "Sirs, what must I do to be saved?" They replied, "Believe in the Lord Jesus and you and your household will be saved." (Acts 16:30-31)

Paul and Barnabas decided to split up. Paul took Timothy and Silas with him to do missionary work.

One day they arrived at a city called Philippi. There was a place just outside the city where people met to pray. They told the crowd about Jesus there.

One day while they were on their way to that place of prayer again, a slave girl followed them. She was shouting because she had a demon in her. Paul drove it out and the girl was healed. Her owners grabbed Paul and Silas and dragged them to the marketplace. The two were beaten up and thrown into prison.

Around midnight, Paul and Silas started praying. Suddenly there was an earthquake. The prison doors flew open. The jailer thought all the prisoners had escaped. He wanted to kill himself. Paul stopped him: "Don't do it! We are all here." Then he talked to the jailer about Jesus.

The jailer took them home with him. He, and everybody in his house, started believing in God.

Remember: Nothing is impossible for the Lord.

Believe in the Lord Jesus!

October 26 Romans 10

If you say with your mouth that Jesus is Lord and believe in your heart that God raised Him from the dead, you will be saved. (Rom. 10:9)

How do we know that someone is a Christian? A Christian is someone who believes that Jesus is Lord and was raised from the dead by God. This is what Paul writes in his letter to the Romans.

A Christian knows that Jesus is not lying in a grave somewhere in Jerusalem. He rose from the dead. He is alive! Jesus is in the best and most important place there is. He rules in heaven over everything and everyone here on earth. He is the King of heaven and earth.

If we believe in Jesus, we know that He has saved us. He makes us children of God. He takes away our sins. He takes care of us every day and He will make sure that we go to heaven someday.

By faith we take Jesus at His word. Faith is believing that He does what He says in the Bible. Faith is knowing that Jesus' blood washed us as white as snow. He forgives every bad thing we do. When we tell Him we're sorry for our sins, He won't think of them ever again because He forgives and forgets.

Remember: Because of Jesus we can live forever.

Paul suffers in Thessalonica

October 27 Acts 17

Paul explained to the people exactly what is written in the Bible. He showed them that the Bible says Christ had to suffer and rise from the dead. (Acts 17:3)

One day Paul and his helpers came to a city called Thessalonica. They went to the synagogue where the Jews worshiped and started telling the people about Jesus.

Some Jews became Christians; others didn't. The Jewish leaders began to get very jealous of Paul when they saw how many people chose to believe in Jesus. They gathered a mob to attack Paul, but they couldn't find Paul and Silas in Jason's house where they were staying. They dragged Jason from his home instead and brought him and some of the other believers before the city council. "Paul and Silas have turned the rest of the world upside down," they shouted. The people of the city turned against the Christians, but Jason promised that they wouldn't make trouble so the city officials allowed them to go. That night after dark, the believers helped Paul and Silas to escape from the city.

Remember: The Lord protects His children.

The faith of the Thessalonian believers

October 28 1 Thessalonians 1

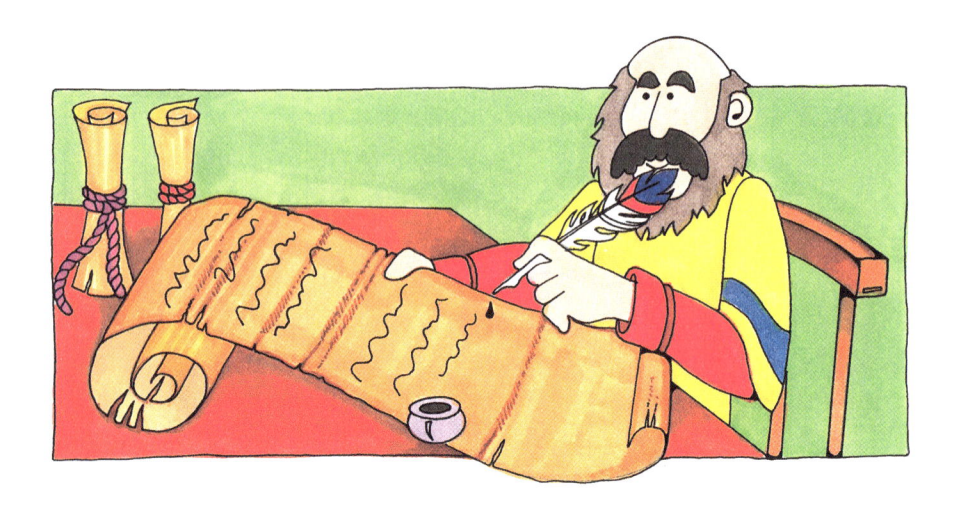

Just like us, you also started believing in the Lord Jesus. Even though you suffered so much, you gave your life to the Lord. The joy that suddenly came into your lives is from the Holy Spirit. (1 Thess. 1:6)

Paul wrote two letters to the believers in Thessalonica. In the first one he tells them how happy he is that they gave their lives to the Lord. Paul says he cannot thank God enough for this.

Paul writes that the believers in Thessalonica lived like true Christians right from the start. It wasn't easy. People made fun of them and said mean things about them, but they didn't let it worry them. All they wanted to do was what Jesus said. Their lives were full of joy. Everybody could see they were brand-new people.

It's really amazing to see how a person's life changes when he or she becomes the Lord's child. We can never be the same once Jesus comes into our lives. We feel, think, and behave differently. Jesus makes us new from head to toe.

Can our friends tell by the way we live that we are the Lord's children? Do we like talking about everything Jesus does for us or are we a bit embarrassed? We should never be ashamed to say we're Christians.

Remember: Jesus brings happiness into our lives.

Don't be mean

October 29 1 Thessalonians 5

See that no one pays back evil for evil, but always try to do good to each other and to everyone else. (1 Thess. 5:15)

Paul writes to the believers in Thessalonica that Christians do not live like unbelievers. Christians are not always watching others to see if they can catch them doing something wrong. Christians forgive each other and don't bear a grudge if someone has treated them badly. They forget about it quickly.

When Jesus is busy working with our lives, He has a large eraser in His hand. Every day He erases out all our sins and He wants us to do the same for other people. We have to make up our minds not to stay angry with people or to pay them back for being unkind or unfriendly to us. We need to tell them we love them even if they treat us badly.

A Christian really cares for others, no matter who they are. We shouldn't sit around waiting for other people to be friendly with us before we're nice to them. We should be the first to smile and show them we care. If we follow what the Bible tells us we'll be friendly and helpful and we'll never forget to pray for them.

Remember: Be kind to others.

Paul preaches in Athens

October 30 Acts 17

When they heard Paul speak of the resurrection of a person who had been dead, some laughed, but others said, "We want to hear more about this later." (Acts 17:32)

One day Paul went to Athens. While he was waiting for his friends he was deeply upset by all the idols he saw in the city. He went to a meeting of the city's leaders to tell what he believed. The Areopagus was a place where one could go and listen to intelligent and well-educated people speak.

Paul told the people of Athens that he could see that they were very religious. As he was walking around in town he saw their many altars. He even saw one with the words "To an Unknown God" on it, and he said that he would like to tell them about this God.

Paul started off by saying that this God doesn't live in manmade temples. He Himself gives life to everything on earth. He gives us what we need. It is because of Him that we live and move and breathe every day.

Then Paul told them that God has appointed Jesus to judge the world. But first He raised Him from the dead. Many people laughed when Paul talked about Jesus coming back to life. Others listened and wanted to know more. Some joined him and became believers.

Remember: Because of Him we live and move and breathe every day.

Paul works in Corinth

October 31 Acts 18

One night the Lord spoke to Paul in a vision and told him, "Don't be afraid! Speak out! Don't be silent! For I am with you, and no one will harm you. Many people in this city belong to Me." (Acts 18:9-10)

Paul left Athens and went to Corinth, where he stayed with a man called Aquila and his wife, Priscilla. They made tents. Paul went to the Jewish synagogue to speak to the people about Jesus.

The leaders paid no attention to Paul, so he left. He went to the house of Titus and preached there.

One night the Lord told Paul not to be afraid. He would take care of him. Paul stayed and worked in Corinth for the next year and a half. When Gallio became the new governor, the Jews tried to bring Paul before him for judgment but Gallio was unimpressed with their accusations and sent them out of the courtroom.

We should ask the Lord every day to protect us and our families. And we should believe that He will. And we should remember to thank Him every night for being with us.

Remember: Nothing happens unless the Lord knows about it.

God's children should not fight

November 1 1 Corinthians 1 & 3

I beg all of you in the Name of the Lord Jesus Christ to stop arguing among yourselves. Be of one mind, in what you think and believe and do. (1 Cor. 1:10)

Paul wrote letters to the Christians in Corinth. He was worried because they were quarreling and fighting with each other. Some Corinthian Christians said they only liked Paul. Others said, "I follow Peter." Yet others said they weren't interested in what people like Paul or Peter said. They would only do what Christ said.

Soon the people of Corinth divided into different groups and each group thought they were the best Christians. Paul wrote to them and told them to stop quarreling. He reminded them that Christians should be like one big family.

Even today many people in the church argue about who is right and who is wrong. The church should be like a family in which every member cares for the other members. The Lord doesn't want us to live only for ourselves and always think we're right. We should love each other and take the time to do things for our friends. We should also try hard to get along with other Christians.

Remember: In God's church we should love each other.

Paul preaches in Ephesus

November 2 Acts 19

In Ephesus the message of the Lord spread widely and had a powerful effect. (Acts 19:20)

When Paul left Corinth he went to Ephesus. He stayed there for almost three years. He preached in the Jewish synagogue for three months. Then he left and rented a building where, for the next two years, he told people about Jesus.

During this time a group of men traveled from town to town casting out evil spirits. When they met a man in Ephesus who had a devil in him, they said, "I command you in the Name of Jesus to come out." The spirit realized that they didn't know Jesus and attacked them. The story of what happened spread quickly throughout Ephesus. The people were frightened. Magicians burned all their books on magic. So the word of the Lord changed the lives of many people.

Because of Paul's preaching, the handmade gods in the temples weren't so popular anymore. The gods in the temple of the goddess Artemis weren't selling well at all. The man who made them, Demetrius, and other craftsmen were losing money. Demetrius organized a protest against Paul but it wasn't successful. The mayor of the city managed to calm the people down.

Remember: The Devil fears the Lord.

November 3 2 Corinthians 1

Paul lands in jail in Ephesus

I think you ought to know what we went through in the province of Asia. We were treated so badly that we started thinking we would not get out of prison alive. (2 Cor. 1:8)

While Paul was working in Ephesus he was sent to prison. There were people in town who were angry with him because he talked to them about Jesus. Paul says this was one of the most difficult times of his life. He was having such a bad time that he started thinking he would never get out of there alive.

The Lord saw Paul's suffering. Just when Paul thought that this was the end, God came to the rescue. Paul writes that it was a great miracle. It was like turning around at death's door. After this experience Paul's faith was even stronger than before. He now knew that God would protect him no matter what kind of trouble he was in.

God cares for all of His children. We should never think He is too busy to help us or that He has forgotten about us. Even if it takes some time for God to answer our prayers, He hears everything we ask Him. Just keep on praying. God is listening. He never sleeps.

Remember: God can help in every problem we have.

Paul holds on to the Lord

November 4 2 Corinthians 4

We are sometimes pushed around. But we never lose heart. People let us down. But the Lord never leaves us. (2 Cor. 4:8)

It isn't always easy to be a follower of the Lord. Ask Paul. Wicked people often hunted him down. He was pushed around and beaten up. Enemies even tried to kill him. Sometimes Paul just didn't know what to do anymore. He was almost like a clay pot, which is easily broken.

No matter how much Paul suffered, he never gave up. He went on doing what the Lord told him to do. How could he do this? He gives us the answer himself. He writes that there was a treasure inside him. This is the Holy Spirit that lived in his heart. Paul also knew that God would never let him down.

Some Christians give up too easily. We shouldn't be like them. God is with us. Even if we feel like an old broken clay pot, we are still in the Lord's hands. Even if we don't always know what to do, He cares for us. Believe it. We need to hold on to the Lord's hand because there is a precious treasure inside us: the Holy Spirit.

Remember: We are precious to the Lord.

Paul's prayer for the church

November 5 Ephesians 3

I pray that you may know how much Christ loves you. His love is so great we will never really understand it. May your whole life be filled with the power that comes from God. (Eph. 3:19)

Paul wrote a letter to the Christians in Ephesus where he had worked for three years. In this letter he prays that God will give them strength, and that they will make a home for Christ in their hearts.

Paul also asks the Lord to help the Ephesians love others. He prays that they will understand how much God loves them and all His other people.

Jesus' love is too great for us to understand, but there is a way we can see how much He loves us. We can see this when we allow His strength to work in our lives. We need to tell God every day that our lives belong to Him. He can steer us any way He wants. Then we will start noticing how powerful and great God is and we will live more like He wants us to live.

Paul ends his prayer by giving all the glory to God because He is so good. He says God is so much greater than we could ever imagine. We cannot even begin to understand how much He is able to do.

Remember: God is much greater than we could ever imagine.

What does a Christian family look like?

November 6 Ephesians 5-6

Children, obey your parents because you belong to the Lord. This is the right thing to do. (Eph. 6:1)

In his letter to the Ephesians Paul also talks to mothers and fathers. He tells them how they should treat each other. Paul tells the children that they should always obey their parents. The Lord expects them to.

Paul tells parents to raise their children the way the Lord wants. If children don't listen, their parents must be strict with them.

Our parents should make sure that we stay on the right path—the Lord's path. That's why they discipline us when we are naughty. Remember that the Lord gave us our parents. We should love them very much and pray for them often. Ask the Lord to take good care of them every day.

We should always listen to our parents. The Lord tells our parents what to do so that we can grow up in the right way. He tells them to take good care of us and He asks us to be good. We need to try to make our parents happy by loving them and the Lord.

Remember: We should pray for our parents every day.

November 7 Ephesians 6

Put on the Lord's armor

We are not fighting against people, but against the Devil and his evil spirits. (E*ph.* 6:12)

Paul says we have a dangerous enemy. This enemy is the Devil. He is always on the lookout for ways to make us do things that are mean and displease God, but the Lord gives us proper uniforms and weapons to protect us in our fight against the Devil.

Our first weapon is a belt of truth. This means we should hold on to Jesus every day. He is the only truth. The steel plate that covers our breast shows that God is on our side. For shoes, we put on the peace that comes from the good news that Jesus died for our sins. We should tell others, who don't know Jesus, this good news.

In every battle we will need faith as our shield. We need to believe in God, all the time. Then the Devil can't harm us. The helmet on our heads is the knowledge that Jesus is our Savior. Our sword is the Bible. What we learn from the Bible helps us chase the Devil away every time he bothers us.

This is the suit of armor that the Lord gives us. We need to wear it every day. We have to pray for the Lord to make us strong so the Devil can't hurt us.

Remember: When we wear Jesus' weapons it scares the Devil.

Jesus is with us through His Spirit

November 8 Ephesians 1

Because you believe in Christ, the Holy Spirit who is from Him has put His stamp on you. This shows that you belong to God alone. (Eph. 1:13)

The Holy Spirit is very important. He is also God, the same as the Father and the Son. The Holy Spirit lives in every Christian. He is the guarantee God gives us that He will do everything He promised. Without the Holy Spirit we can't be Christians.

The Holy Spirit sees to it that we listen to God. He also makes sure we get to heaven one day. That's why He is like a stamp or a seal on our lives. An official document or certificate often has a seal on it to show that it's genuine. A certificate belongs to the person to whom it was awarded. In a similar way, the Lord puts a seal on our lives to say we belong to Him. This seal is the Holy Spirit.

The Holy Spirit tells us we are God's children. We are on our way to Him. He puts His stamp on our lives and it won't come off.

Remember: God puts His stamp on our lives. It won't come off.

All Christians are important to God

November 9 Galatians 3

When you belong to the Lord it makes no difference what language you speak. It doesn't matter if you are rich or poor, a girl or a boy. All who believe in Jesus are one big family. (Gal. 3:28)

Some people think they're more important than others. Some children think they are better than others because they have more money or more clothes. The Lord doesn't care about things like that. He doesn't need to know what you own before He decides to love you. It makes no difference to Him what language you speak, or whether you are a boy or a girl. The Lord loves everybody. He has no favorites.

It's the same in our churches. All Christians are important to the Lord. In Jesus' eyes we are one big family. All of us who believe in Him are brothers and sisters. He is the Head of the family and our Lord. Jesus takes care of us, every day, because He loves us very much.

Jesus doesn't like us to think that we're better or smarter than others. We shouldn't think too much of ourselves but love all the Lord's children.

Remember: Other Christians are our brothers and sisters.

The temple of the Holy Spirit

November 10 1 Corinthians 6

Don't you know that your body is the temple of the Holy Spirit, who lives in you and was given to you by God? You do not belong to yourselves anymore. (1 Cor. 6:19)

A Christian is someone who has been bought at a high price. God bought each one of us and paid for us with Jesus' blood. From head to toe we belong to Him.

After God had bought us He sent the Holy Spirit to each of us. The Holy Spirit lives in us and so our bodies become a temple. The Holy Spirit changes our lives so that we can be a temple for God to live in. We need to give our lives to the Holy Spirit, every day. He will do the rest.

When we believe in Jesus we aren't our own bosses anymore. We belong to Him because He bought us. That's why we need to ask the Lord before we say or do something. We can't do or say just what we want but only what the Lord tells us to.

Remember: Jesus bought us. We are His.

Paul speaks to the Ephesian elders

November 11 Acts 20

"Let me speak plainly: it is not my fault if any of you are not saved. I have told you exactly how God saves sinners." (Acts 20:26-27)

Once when Paul was on his way to Jerusalem, he stayed at Troas where he talked to all the believers one Sunday night. Paul spoke for a very long time and a young man named Eutychus fell asleep. He was sitting on a windowsill and he fell out of the window, which was three stories up. When they picked him up he was dead. Paul went down, bent over Eutychus, and took him in his arms. Then he said to the people, "Don't worry, he's alive!" And sure enough, the young man got up and went home, unhurt.

The next part of the journey was by ship. When Paul arrived in Miletus he decided to stay there for a while. He sent a message to the elders in Ephesus to visit him there. When they arrived, Paul told them that they would never see him again. They had to remember every word he taught them about Jesus, and they had to have faith in Him. He told the elders to watch over the believers and help them follow God.

Remember: Always have faith in the Lord.

We should care for one another

November 12 Acts 20

"You must remember the words of the Lord Jesus: 'It is more blessed to give than to receive.'" (Acts 20:35)

Paul reminded the Ephesian elders that he had never taken any money from them. When he stayed with them, he made tents for a living. Christians should follow his example. They shouldn't sit around, expecting other people to give them what they need. They need to help each other.

Paul says Christians should care for each other and those who have a lot should help those who don't have as much.

Jesus says it's better to give than to receive. He gave us His life. The least we can do is to share our time, our money, and our possessions with others. That will please the Lord.

Selfish Christians, who hold on to their possessions without caring for poor people, are not good "advertisements" for God's love. We should open up our lives to God's goodness and share our blessings with others.

Remember: We should never boast about what we have.

We are part of Christ's body on earth

November 13 1 Corinthians 12

Now all of you together are Christ's body, and each one of you is a separate and necessary part of it. (1 Cor. 12:27)

Paul tells us that as Christians we are the Lord's body here on earth. A body is made up of different parts and if one part of our body isn't working, we get sick. When we have a cold, or if we break a leg, our whole body feels it.

Every Christian is part of Christ's body. One is the mouth, another is the eyes, yet another is a finger and another the ears. And every Christian, every single little part of Jesus' body, is important. Because if just one small part doesn't work, the rest of the body feels it. If one Christian says, "Oh well, the church doesn't need me," then the body of Christ doesn't work as well as it should.

We are part of Christ's body here on earth. Jesus wants to use us so the rest of His body can stay healthy and strong. We need to do our part. We should pray regularly, read our Bible, and care for other Christians. In this way we help to keep Christ's body healthy.

Remember: Each believer is an important part of Jesus' body.

Paul is arrested in Jerusalem

November 14 Acts 21

Some Jews from the province of Asia saw Paul in the temple and got a crowd together. They grabbed Paul, yelling, "Men of Israel! Help! This is the man who teaches against our people and the temple and the laws of Moses. He has brought people of all nations into our temple. He fills our holy place with sin!" (Acts 21:27-28)

Paul went to Jerusalem to pray in the temple. When he arrived in the city he went first to visit Jesus' brother, James. James and a few elders of the church asked Paul to help out four men who were there for a religious ceremony. Would Paul pay for their offerings?

At the temple, some Jews recognized him. They were angry when they saw him there and thought he had just come to find fault with them. This was not true, of course, but they started yelling and stirring up the other Jews so that eventually they all turned against Paul. They dragged him out of the temple in order to kill him outside the city gates.

The commander of the Roman army in Jerusalem saw what was happening. He immediately sent his soldiers to arrest Paul and take him to a building next to the temple.

Remember: Trust in the Lord.

Paul defends himself

November 15 Acts 22-23

The Lord said to Paul, "Leave Jerusalem. I am sending you far away. You must go to people who are not Jewish." (Acts 22:21)

The crowd at the temple in Jerusalem wanted to kill Paul, but the Roman soldiers saved him. Before they locked him up Paul asked the commander, "Please let me talk to these people."

Paul told the crowd about the day Jesus spoke to him on the road to Damascus and how this had changed his whole life. He became a Christian then and there. Afterwards he came back to Jerusalem. In the temple he saw a vision of Jesus telling him to get out of Jerusalem. The Lord told Paul that the Jews wouldn't believe him.

The Jewish crowd was furious. They shouted, "Kill him!" The soldiers locked him up in prison just in time.

The next day Paul was brought before the Jewish high court. When he said he believed in the resurrection of the dead, the people started fighting again. They shouted and started tugging at Paul so he was locked up again. The commander then sent Paul to Caesarea before the Jews could kill him.

Remember: The Lord makes people new.

Paul before Felix

November 16 Acts 24

Paul said to the Roman governor Felix, "These men certainly cannot prove the things they accuse me of doing." (Acts 24:13)

When Paul arrived in Caesarea he was taken to Governor Felix. He stayed in prison until his case was heard. A few days later, the Jewish leaders arrived to press charges against Paul. They told Governor Felix that Paul was a danger to other people.

Paul answered that he worshiped the God of his ancestors, just like all Jews. But Felix had him locked up anyway.

Paul was in prison in Caesarea for two years. During this time Felix often sent for Paul. Paul talked to him and his wife about God. He told them that we should obey God and not sin. Paul also warned them that God was coming back to the world one day and sinners would be punished.

Paul was not afraid to witness for Christ, even if it meant sitting in jail for two years. We shouldn't be afraid to talk to our friends about Jesus either. We shouldn't feel embarrassed to say we belong to Jesus. We should talk about Him, no matter what!

Remember: Christians like to talk about Jesus.

Jesus is the greatest

November 17 Philippians 2

At the Name of Jesus every knee will bow, in heaven and on earth. All will say, "Jesus Christ is Lord! Then God's Name will be glorified." (Phil. 2:10-11)

Jesus is more important than anybody or anything in the whole world. Before He came down to earth, all the angels bowed before Him. They worshiped Him all day long. But Jesus decided to become an ordinary human being. He took off His heavenly crown and came to live among us.

Jesus knows we are all sinners. It is impossible for us to reach God on our own. That is why Jesus decided to give His life away for our sake.

After the death and resurrection of Jesus, God gave Him the most important place in heaven. Jesus was also given the most important Name in the world. His Name is Lord! Everyone who hears this Name must bow before Him. Everyone must say Jesus is the ruler of the whole world.

We who believe in Jesus bow before Him every day. It's good to know He is our Lord.

Remember: Jesus is our Lord.

Jesus has the whole world in His hands

November 18 Colossians 1

Jesus, the Son of God, is the image of the God we cannot see. Jesus is more important than anybody else. He is the ruler over all creation. (Col. 1:15)

Paul wrote a beautiful song about the Lord, saying how great and powerful He is. Jesus is the image of God. He is the most important Person in creation. Jesus was there when God created everything. Through Him, God created everything we can see with our eyes, as well as everything we cannot see. Jesus also made all the angels. They are there to serve Him.

Ever since the very beginning, before there was anything or anyone in the world, Jesus was already there. He takes care of the whole world.

We should bow before Jesus every day. He loves us very much. He gave His life for us so that we can be God's children forever. We need to serve Him every day and remember that Jesus is the most important Person in the whole world.

Remember: Jesus takes care of our families every day.

November 19 Romans 6

Jesus has known us a long time

The prize for sinning is the same for everyone: death! But God gives a wonderful prize to all who believe. He gives us the free gift of everlasting life because we believe Jesus Christ is Lord. (Rom. 6:23)

Sin is a terrible thing. It destroys lives. But there is good news. Paul tells us that sinners are given a lousy first prize for their trouble. This prize is death! Those who don't want to listen to God will be in hell forever.

God knew that we could never reach out to Him on our own. We're too sinful for that. We can do nothing to please Him and we must be punished for our sins. But if we believe in Jesus, we won't go to hell. God gives us His own first prize—everlasting life! All His children will live with Him forever. He takes us directly to Him in heaven.

Only those who believe can win God's prize. Only His children can live with Him forever because He forgives His children all their sins.

Remember: The first prize awarded to believers is eternal life.

I don't like sin at all

November 20 Colossians 2 & 3

Because you belong to Christ, you have been made new. It is not people who made you new, but Christ. He took away your sinful nature. (Col. 2:11)

Jesus came to do something wonderful in our lives. He took our sinful hearts away because we believe in Him. Jesus doesn't save us and then forget all about us. He makes us brand-new people from head to toe.

Paul tells the Christians in Colossae that Jesus performed an operation on us. He cut out our sinful hearts. We don't belong to the Devil any more. We are really free because Jesus took all our sins away.

Paul says that Jesus nailed every one of our sins to the cross with Him. Then His blood flowed over them and washed everything clean. He can't see our sins anymore—we are free.

As children of Jesus, we don't like sin so we tell the Devil "no" when he wants us to do or think bad things.

Remember: Jesus has given each one of us a new heart.

Jesus lives in me

November 21 Galatians 2

I *myself no longer live, but Christ lives in me. So I live my life on earth, trusting in the Son of God. He loves me and gave Himself for me.* (Gal. 2:20)

When Jesus died on the cross, we died with Him. And when He rose from the dead on the third day, we were raised with Him. We're dead to sin now. The Devil can't do what he wants to with us anymore.

Paul said that once Jesus lives in us we can't do what we want with our lives anymore. We belong to Him so we need to listen to Him every day. Jesus decides what we should do and say and think every day.

Jesus loves us very much. He didn't just send a message down from heaven to say He still loves us. He came to us Himself. He died so that we can live forever.

Believing in Jesus is the most important thing we can ever do. We believe in Jesus because He made us His children. We believe in Him because He died on the cross in our place and gives us everlasting life.

Remember: We belong to Jesus.

Jesus has a place for each of us in heaven

November 22 Philippians 3

We are all citizens of heaven, where the Lord Jesus Christ lives. One of these days He will come back to get us. (Phil. 3:20)

We are citizens of heaven. We are going to live with Jesus forever. Paul wrote that this is the reason why God never stops working in our lives. He will finish His good work in our lives. He will make sure we believe in Him until Jesus comes back to us someday.

We are all citizens of the country we live in. It gives us certain privileges and special rights that citizens of other countries don't have. There is something much more important than being a citizen of our country, and that is being a citizen of heaven.

Because we believe in Jesus, we won't end up among the sinners in hell. Jesus will come and get us so we can be with Him forever. A child of the Lord is not afraid of death because Jesus is stronger than death. Jesus was the winner and death was the loser.

Every day we should live in such a way that everybody can see we are citizens of heaven. Others should see that we are happy because Jesus has given us everlasting life.

Remember: Some day we are going to live with Jesus.

Athletes on Jesus' team

November 23 1 Corinthians 9

Remember that in a race everyone runs, but only one person can win. He gets the prize. Run for the Lord in such a way that you will win. (1 Cor. 9:24)

In a race there can only be one winner. Every athlete runs to win. Paul says the Lord's athletes should also run to get first place, and the Bible has good news for all athletes on Jesus' team. Everyone who runs his or her best for Jesus is a winner. Everyone who pays attention to what the Bible says takes first place in the Lord's eyes.

An athlete has to practice hard to do well. A lazy athlete who doesn't exercise will never win a medal. We need to practice hard if we want to run a good race for the Lord. We have to pray often and read our Bible. A good athlete is willing to practice hard even when he or she doesn't feel like it. We should also be willing to work for the Lord even when it's difficult.

We have a very good coach—Jesus. He knows exactly how we should run. We just need to do what He tells us to win an awesome prize—everlasting life!

Remember: Run a good race for Jesus.

Be happy—The Lord is with you

November 24 Philippians 4

Always be full of joy in the Lord. I say it again—rejoice! (Phil. 4:4)

It wasn't always easy for Paul to be a Christian. Sometimes he ended up in prison. At times people threw stones at him and beat him up, but he never stopped believing. No matter how difficult it was, Paul never gave up. When he wrote to the Philippians, he was in prison for talking to people about Jesus. But being imprisoned couldn't take away his joy.

Paul wrote that Christians must always be joyful. This isn't hard to do, because God is a wonderful God. He loves us so much that He sent His only Son to us. But that's not all. God also sent the Holy Spirit to come and live in us. We're never alone and we are going to live forever, with God.

We have lots of reasons to be joyful every day. God does so much for us. Nothing that happens to us can take us away from God. Not even the Devil is strong enough to steal us from Him.

Let's think of a few reasons for being joyful today, and then tell our parents and thank the Lord!

Remember: We should be glad because Jesus is with us.

Talk to the Lord— He is listening

November 25 Philippians 4

Don't worry about anything; instead, pray about everything. Tell God what you need, and thank Him for all He has done. (Phil. 4:6)

Prayer is truly amazing. Just think—we can speak to the most important Person in the whole world every day and, best of all, He really listens to us. He hears every word we say. God is never too busy for His children. He makes time to listen to all of our prayers.

We need to pray regularly. Paul says we can talk to God about anything. Nothing in our hearts is too small or too unimportant for Him. We can take everything to Him in prayer.

Prayer is no joke. We don't pray out of habit. Praying is speaking to God Himself, and we need to believe that He hears us and will answer our prayers. We have to remember to thank Him for taking the time to listen!

Prayer is not just giving God a wish list. Prayer is saying thank you to God for being so great. Prayer should not be all about us, but about God. When we pray like this, then we're not afraid or worried anymore. We believe that God will help us.

Remember: Talk to God every day.

Paul before Festus and Agrippa

November 26 Acts 25 & 26

King Agrippa said to Paul, "Do you think you can make me a Christian so quickly?" Paul replied, "Whether quickly or not, I pray that both you and everyone here in this audience might become the same as I am...." (Acts 26:28-29)

Paul was in prison in Caesarea for a long time. During that time a new Roman governor took over. His name was Festus. He wanted the Jewish leaders in Jerusalem on his side. So he decided to transfer Paul to Jerusalem for his trial. But Paul refused. He was a Roman citizen and it was his right to be heard by Caesar in Rome.

While Paul was waiting to go to Rome, the Jewish king Agrippa arrived in Caesarea. "I'd like to hear the man speak," Agrippa said. Many people arrived at the place where Paul was going to talk to King Agrippa about God. Paul told him how he became a Christian. At one stage Paul asked the king, "King Agrippa, do you believe?" But Agrippa didn't want to become a Christian.

Afterwards Agrippa told some people that Paul was not guilty. He didn't deserve to be in prison.

Remember: Pray for somebody who doesn't believe in Jesus.

Paul on a sinking ship

November 27 Acts 27

The angel said, "Don't be afraid, Paul. You will stand trial before Caesar! What's more, because you are on this ship, God will spare the lives of everyone sailing with you." (Acts 27:24)

Roman soldiers took Paul to Rome on a ship. On the way there Paul warned them that a bad storm was heading their way. He saw trouble ahead if they went on. The ship might be damaged.

No one on the ship paid any attention to Paul. The captain just sailed on. Then the weather changed suddenly. A mighty storm was brewing. The strong wind blew the ship off course. Eventually the crew began throwing cargo overboard to make the ship lighter.

Then one night an angel came to Paul and stood beside him. He told Paul that God would save the lives of everybody on board. God wanted Paul to appear before Caesar in Rome.

After the ship had been drifting on the sea for 14 days, the sailors saw land. They headed for the shore, but the ship hit some rocks. The ship broke apart but no one died. Everybody on the ship swam safely ashore!

God keeps His word. He cares for us so much that He holds our lives in His hand. Sometimes He saves us from great danger. We should thank Him for taking care of us every day.

Remember: We need to listen to what we are told about God in church.

Snakebite on the Island of Malta

November 28 Acts 28

As Paul was putting wood on the fire, a poisonous snake bit him on the hand. The people of the island saw it hanging from Paul's hand and said, "This man is a murderer. He has just been saved from the sea, but the gods won't stop punishing him." But Paul shook off the snake into the fire. He was not hurt. (Acts 28:3-5)

Paul and the others were washed up on the island of Malta. It was cold, so they built a fire. A snake hidden in a pile of wood bit Paul on the hand. Paul just shook it off. He wasn't hurt.

Afterwards Paul visited the chief of the island. His name was Publius. Publius' father was sick with a fever. Paul prayed for him and he was healed.

Paul was not ashamed to live for Christ and the Lord used him in many different ways and places. In prisons he led people to Jesus. At sea, when the ship was about to sink, it was because of Paul that God saved the lives of everybody on the ship.

We should never think that the Lord can't use us because we're too young. Age doesn't matter to Him. We can put our hand into His strong hand, and leave the rest to Him.

Remember: Live for God anywhere you are.

Paul arrives in Rome

November 29 Acts 28

Paul told the people in Rome about God's new world. He taught them all about the Lord Jesus Christ. He did this without fear. And no one tried to stop him. (Acts 28:31)

After three months on the island of Malta, Paul left for Rome with the Roman soldiers. The Christians in Rome were very glad to see Paul.

The Romans allowed Paul to live in his own rented house. A soldier guarded him. Three days after Paul arrived in Rome, he invited the local Jewish leaders to his home. He talked to them about Jesus but they wouldn't listen to him. Paul told them that was why God sent him to other nations, because his own people, the Jews, were not interested in Jesus.

One person can make a difference! The Lord doesn't need lots of people to change the world. One person who obeys Him can do a lot. Take Paul. The Lord used him to tell people all over the world about Jesus. Nothing or nobody could keep him quiet. Even to this day we hear his voice in all the wonderful letters he wrote. If we read them often, we will get to know God well and discover all the wonderful things that Paul wrote about God for ourselves.

Remember: We are important to the Lord. He wants to use us.

The best good news there is

November 30 Romans 1

I am not ashamed of this good news about Christ. It is the power of God at work, saving everyone who believes. (Rom. 1:16)

In the letter Paul wrote to the Christians in Rome, he explains all about the good news. He says God is not an angry God, ready and waiting to punish people. God is on the lookout for sinners, but He wants to make them His children. God didn't make people so they'd end up in hell. He wants us all to be with Him in His heavenly home.

God uses ordinary people to tell others the good news. He doesn't use angels. His agents are people like us—not people with some kind of super powers, and not just adults. He uses everybody who says Jesus is the Lord of his or her life.

Every Christian is a witness for the Lord. It's our job to spread the news that God loves sinners. We don't have to pass an exam to do this. We don't need to know the Bible by heart either. All we need to do is to tell our friends and other people that Jesus loves them. He gives everlasting life to everyone who believes, for free! We should tell Jesus we are sorry for our sins and leave our lives in His hands.

Remember: Tell others about eternal life with Jesus.

God cares

December 1 Romans 5

God is not angry with us about our sins anymore. Because we now believe in Jesus Christ. So now we have peace with God because of what Jesus Christ our Lord has done for us. (Rom. 5:1)

There are people who are afraid of God. They think He is only interested in punishing them for their sins. Paul says, "that's not true!" If we belong to the Lord, He has taken away all our sins. Jesus has already taken the punishment for our sins.

God isn't angry with His children anymore because Jesus paid the price for our sins. That means we're free now. We have peace with God. He isn't interested in punishing us.

There is no reason for us to be afraid of the Lord. Of course we should have respect for Him, but God is also our Father. He made peace with us and we are His children, no matter what we do. He loves us just the way we are.

The blood of Jesus washed us clean. God knows us as His children, not as a bunch of sinners. We have to thank the Lord every day that we are His children.

Remember: The blood of Jesus washed us clean.

Peter also does missionary work

December 2 1 Corinthians 9

We have the right to bring our wives along with us when we do missionary work. The other disciples and the Lord's brothers and Peter all do it. (1 Cor. 9:5)

Paul wasn't the only person who did missionary work. Many other Christians also brought the good news to people. Before long, people all over the world knew about Jesus. The small group of believers who waited for the Holy Spirit after Jesus' crucifixion soon grew to thousands of people.

Peter started preaching the gospel far away from Jerusalem. He was head of the church in Jerusalem for a while, but then he decided it was part of his job to preach the gospel in other places as well.

Paul tells us that Peter took his wife along on his missionary journeys. They worked in Corinth and also in Rome. Just like Paul, Peter wasn't embarrassed to talk about Jesus. His faith was all that mattered to him. Peter traveled many miles on foot. He wanted to make sure that as many people as possible would get the chance to hear that Jesus saves them from death.

Remember: We are all missionaries for Jesus.

Peter's letters: Live the way Jesus wants you to

December 3 1 Peter 1

You were born again when you became Christians. But this new life will last forever. (1 Pet. 1:23)

Peter wrote a few letters to other Christians. In his first letter he says that believers should always listen to God and love each other. This is what God expects us to do.

Peter goes on to say that Christians are born a second time. The first time is when we are born into the world as babies. The second time is when we become Christians. This is just like starting life for the first time.

When we become God's children we are given a new heart—a complete makeover. We are new people, and we need to live a new life because we have been completely changed.

We belong to the Lord so we are no longer the slaves of sin. We can tell the Devil that we don't want to do bad things. We can do what Jesus wants us to, every day.

Remember: We are children of God.

We are Jesus' new home

December 4 1 Peter 2

You must allow God to use you as living bricks. Let Him build you so that all of you form a new home. You must belong to God only. Like priests you must serve Him. Bring spiritual sacrifices that please Him through Jesus Christ. (1 Pet. 2:5)

A house is built with bricks, and so is the church of Jesus. There is one difference though—Jesus uses only living bricks. He uses His children. Jesus doesn't live in a church building but in people. He lives in everybody who believes in Him.

Jesus wants us to be living bricks that He can use to put up a great building for God. Christians together should be a temple—one that God can be proud of. For Him to be able to do this, Jesus asks us to place our lives in His hands every day so He can use us as He wants.

If we decide for ourselves what God's temple should look like, and try to do the building ourselves, we are never going to please the Lord. But if we're willing to wait until He decides to build us into God's temple where He wants to, then we will please Him. We are like priests who bring offerings that glorify the Name of the Lord.

Remember: We are a living house for the Lord.

Don't be afraid of suffering

December 5 1 Peter 4

Be happy if you are insulted for being a Christian. This shows that the Holy Spirit of God is with you. (1 Pet. 4:14)

Here Peter is writing to Christians who were suffering. People who didn't believe in Jesus were giving these Christians a hard time. They were upset. When Peter heard about it he wrote to them, telling them not to be discouraged—Christians sometimes suffer.

Jesus didn't say it would be easy being His children. He knows that wicked people don't like Christians. If others make fun of us because we believe in Jesus, Peter says we should be pleased because it proves that we are living for Jesus. It shows that the Holy Spirit is working in our lives.

When others make fun of us because we belong to Jesus, we shouldn't try to get them back. That's not what God wants. He wants us to pray for them and to remember what Jesus said. Those who believe in Him will sometimes suffer. It pleases the Lord if we take it without complaining. Jesus will keep us safe and fill our lives with His love.

Remember: Walk with Jesus every day.

God is with you, even if others don't like you

December 6   1 Peter 4

Christians who are suffering because it is God's will must trust their lives to God. He created heaven and earth. He will be with you. Just keep on doing what is right. (1 Pet. 4:19)

Peter goes on speaking to Christians who suffer. We should not even think of letting go of God's hand. If we obey God, He will show us the right way, no matter how difficult it might be.

Peter also tells us to remember that when we have problems God is with us. He is more powerful than anyone or anything in the whole world. Nobody is as great and holy as He is.

When we're suffering we shouldn't sit around and mope and feel sorry for ourselves. We should just go on living like children of the Lord. We need to keep doing good works for those around us.

Christians who feel sorry for themselves aren't very useful to Jesus. We need to pray for others and help those who are even worse off than we are. That will help us forget about our own problems.

Remember: We should always be kind to our friends.

Believers never think too highly of themselves

December 7 1 Peter 5

You youngsters, listen to adults. And all of you, old and young, don't think too highly of yourselves. Remember God doesn't like people who think they are better than others. He likes people who are humble. (1 Pet. 5:5)

In church, children still respect grown-ups and adults don't consider themselves better than children. Members of a church care for each other. When someone is having a hard time, other Christians reach out to them. Christians are never too busy to lend a helping hand.

Peter says Christians don't think too highly of themselves. At school and in the adult world people always want to be the best and the smartest and the most successful. But it's different in a church community. Christians there don't brag about themselves. They let the spotlight fall on others.

Our job is to brag about Jesus. We should tell others how great Jesus is. He makes people's lives brand-new. We need to remind our Christian friends how the Lord changed their lives. And we should rejoice with them about this.

The Lord doesn't like people who think they're better than others. He wants us to be humble. We need to bow before Him and respect others.

Remember: Be humble like Jesus.

Don't listen to lies about Jesus

December 8 2 Peter 2

There have always been false prophets, just as there will be false teachers among you. They will twist the message of the gospel cleverly. They will even turn against their Master who bought them. They are all on their way to their death. (2 Pet. 2:1)

There are people who don't preach the gospel correctly or live the way they should. They twist things around to suit themselves. Peter warns us against people like that. He says there have always been dishonest people who say they work for God. These people are going to be punished. They will be judged someday.

How do we know when someone is lying about Jesus? We should turn to the Bible and see what it says. Then we'll know what is true and what is false. If someone says something that isn't in the Bible, we'll know that he or she is wrong. We shouldn't listen to that person. When people talk about things we can find in the Bible, then we should listen to them.

We need to pray every day that people who talk about Jesus will tell the whole truth and that no one will say things about Jesus that aren't true.

Remember: What the Bible says is true.

The Lord is coming soon

December 9 2 Peter 3

Scoffers will say, "Jesus promised to come back, didn't He? Then where is He? Why, as far back as I can remember, everything has remained exactly the same since the world was first created." (2 Pet. 3:4)

Peter heard that some people were making fun of Christians. They were saying that Christians are lying when they tell people Jesus will come back to us. Nothing has changed. Everything is the same as it has always been. People come and go, but the Lord does not come back.

Peter answered these mockers by saying that the Lord is on His way but He wants sinners to repent before He comes back. Otherwise they will all go to hell, where all wicked people will stay forever. God doesn't want that to happen. He didn't make people so they could go to hell. He made people to go to heaven.

We need to invite others to know Jesus. We need to tell them how much Jesus loves them. We need to keep telling people the good news until the day Jesus comes back. We shouldn't worry about when the Lord will come. We should just keep on inviting people to be ready.

Remember: We need to invite our friends to believe in Jesus.

To the Lord, a day is like a thousand years

December 10 2 Peter 3

You must not forget: A day is like a thousand years to the Lord, and a thousand years is like a day. (2 Pet. 3:8)

The Lord's time isn't the same as ours. To Him a full thousand years passes like an hour, and He can stretch an hour to a thousand years.

We often want the Lord to have the same plans as we do. We expect Him to give us an answer to our prayers right away. We want Him to open up heaven when we say so. This is wrong. The Lord doesn't need to make His time fit in with ours. Instead, we need to fall in with His time. We need to learn to wait until the time is right for the Lord.

We shouldn't worry that the Second Coming hasn't taken place yet. The Lord will come back in His own good time. All He asks us to do is to wait patiently. We shouldn't start doing bad things because the Lord wants to wait a little longer before He comes back to earth. His return to earth will be unexpected. Nobody can tell exactly when it will happen.

We should wait for the Lord every day and learn to be patient until He answers our prayers. We can't force Him into something that we want.

Remember: Jesus will definitely come back to us again.

God gives only good things

December 11 James 1

Whatever is good and perfect comes to us from God above.... (James 1:16)

James, the brother of Jesus, also wrote a letter in the Bible. James says if we get caught up in sin, we have only ourselves to blame. It isn't God's fault. Sin is like a tiny seed. If we allow it to start growing in our lives, it can become a giant plant and eventually destroy us.

Sin isn't from God. The bad things that happen in life don't come from Him. It is people who do wicked things. They steal, kill others, and use bad language. God only gives us good things. Life and joy come from God. He opens up His hand and gives us everything that is good.

We should never allow sin to grow like a plant in our lives. We need to stop it in time and never even think of bad things. We should fill our minds with thoughts of Jesus every day and think about what we read in the Bible. If we pray every day then sin cannot win.

Remember—sin starts in our heads. When we start thinking about bad things we are a step away from doing them. So, we need to give our thoughts to the Lord every day.

Remember: God isn't responsible for the wrong things we do.

Do what the Lord says

December 12 James 2

What's the use of saying you have faith if you don't prove it by what you do? That kind of faith can't save anyone. (James 2:14)

Faith is doing. It's not just something we talk about on a Sunday in church. We act out our faith from Monday to Saturday as well as on Sundays. We need to do what the Lord says seven days a week.

James writes that some churchgoers say they believe but he sees no sign of it in their lives. They talk a lot, but do nothing.

James gives an example. He says if you see another believer who is hungry or who needs clothes, it doesn't do any good to say, "Well, goodbye and God bless you. Stay warm and eat well." Faith is doing something about it. Give that person food or clothing. Talk is cheap. It can't take hunger and cold away.

James also uses Abraham as an example. He was willing to offer his son Isaac on the altar when the Lord told him to. It was his faith that made him do whatever God told him.

Faith without action is dead. It means nothing to the Lord. Faith that makes us do what the Lord says is alive.

Remember: Faith that makes us do what the Lord says is alive.

December 13 James 3

God's children say nice things

The tongue is like a fire. It is full of wickedness that can ruin your whole life. From the beginning to the end of your life, your tongue is dangerous. (James 3:6)

James warns us not to speak before thinking. He says our tongues are dangerous. Although the tongue is a small part of our body, it can destroy us. It's like the rudder of a huge ship. It steers the ship any way it wants to.

We can hurt people by the words we say. When we make fun of our friends or say mean things to them, it's like stabbing them with a knife. It's even worse if we say these things behind someone's back.

James says we need to watch what we say. We should ask God to put a guard over our mouths. We want Him to stop us from saying things we'll be sorry about later.

We can't say nice things to God one minute, and the next call somebody else names! Blessing and cursing can't come pouring out of the same mouth. Our words should make others feel better and they should praise the Lord.

Remember: We need to be careful about what we say every day.

The Lord listens when we pray

December 14 James 5

Are any of you suffering? Keep on praying. And those who have reason to be thankful should praise the Lord. (James 5:13)

Prayer works. It is speaking to God Himself, and we should pray often. If we're having a bad time, we don't have to struggle with our problems all by ourselves. We can talk to God about it and ask Him to help us. And when we are happy we should tell the Lord and thank Him.

We should pray when things go wrong and when they go well.

When we're sick we can ask the Lord to make us better and thank Him for making us well again.

There is nothing in our lives that we can't talk to God about. No problem is too small. He invites us to pray and He listens when we do.

Remember: We need to pray every day.

December 15 Jude 1

Watch out for wicked people

Watch out for wicked people who have wormed their way into your church. They think they can live sinful lives because God forgives them every time. They have turned against our only Master and Lord, Jesus Christ. (Jude 1:4)

Jesus had four brothers. Two of them, James and Jude, wrote letters that are in the Bible. Jude tells us in his letter how wicked people sneak into the church. They try to confuse other Christians. These people tell believers that it's all right to sin. They say that the Lord doesn't mind because He forgives our sins anyway.

Jude warns us to be very careful of these people. They twist what is written in the Bible to suit themselves and the way they live. They don't really do what the Lord says. They even insult the angels and God.

Our God is so good to us. But it doesn't mean we can live however we want to live. We have to say "no" to sin. And if we've done something wrong, we have to tell the Lord we're sorry. We need to ask Him to forgive us and we shouldn't do the same thing again.

Sin is like cancer. It keeps on spreading if it isn't treated in time. Treat it with the best "medicine" in the world—the power of the Spirit!

Remember: Say "no" to doing bad things.

The Lord will take care of us until the end

December 16 Jude 1

And now, all glory to God, who is able to keep you from stumbling. You will stand before Him one day with great joy in your heart. Praise Him, He alone is our God, through Jesus Christ our Lord. Yes, He is powerful, mighty and important. He is the greatest, now, and for evermore. (Jude 1:24-25)

Only the Lord is important. The Lord has always lived and He will live forever and ever. He is the most powerful of all, the greatest. There is nobody like Him.

The good news the Bible tells us is that the Lord cares for us as well. He, who is so great and mighty, is interested in us. He takes us in His arms and takes care of us every single day. He makes sure that we are safe.

The Lord will not allow the Devil to take us from Him. He walks alongside us every day. He is with us every step of the way. Isn't this wonderful news? To think that the most important Person in the whole wide world cares for us! To think that He wants us to come and live with Him forever!

Remember: God keeps us close to Him every day.

Jesus is more important than angels

December 17 Hebrews 1

God calls His angels "messengers as fast as the wind; servants made of flaming fire." But to His Son He says, "Your throne, O God, will last forever and ever. You are a fair king." (Heb. 1:7-8)

Angels are very important. They work for the Lord. But Jesus is more important than all the angels put together. The Lord made angels. They worship Him day and night.

Sometimes angels come down to earth to do certain things for God. They obey Him.

Jesus isn't just another important angel. He is the Son of God. Jesus is God Himself. There is a huge difference between Jesus and the angels. That's why God also calls Jesus God. He is quite different to all the other powers in heaven.

Jesus is King of the whole world. He reigns forever. Jesus has the whole world in His hands. We are alive because Jesus wants us to live. We have nothing without Him.

We need to worship Jesus because He is the Son of God. He is the King of the whole world forever and ever.

Remember: We worship Jesus because He is the Son of God.

Jesus broke the power of the Devil

December 18 Hebrews 2

Because God's children are human beings, Jesus also became a human being. He did it to destroy the power of the Devil. It was only as a human being that He could die, and only by dying could He break the power of the Devil, who had the power of death. (Heb. 2:14)

The Devil is not in charge on earth anymore. He has been defeated. This happened when Jesus came to earth. Jesus became a human being because He felt very sorry for all of us. He saw how scared we were of death. That is why He gave His life for us. He came to defeat death. Now death is not our enemy any more because Jesus is stronger than death. He went straight through death and came out the other side alive.

The day we die, Jesus will be there, waiting for us. He will carry us through death to His Father's house. That's why Christians aren't afraid of dying anymore.

Jesus knows exactly what we are thinking. He also knows what scares us. That's why He can help us. He takes care of us and stops the Devil from getting us into his clutches. Jesus is always with us.

Remember: Jesus is always with us.

Jesus is our new high priest

December 19 Hebrews 3-4

We have a very important High Priest: Jesus the Son of God, who has gone to heaven. Let us cling to Him and never stop trusting Him. This High Priest of ours understands our weaknesses, because the Devil also tempted Him, but He did not sin. (Heb. 4:14-15)

In the Old Testament the high priest was the most important priest. It was his job to go into the holiest part of the temple once a year on behalf of the people. The high priest had to bring an offering for the sins of his people.

We read in Hebrews that Jesus is now our new High Priest. He is not like an earthly high priest who has to bring an offering for his own sins first. Jesus is without sin. An earthly priest was only allowed in the most holy part of the temple once a year. But Jesus is in heaven where He will live forever. He is in the most important place in the whole world all the time. That's why He can really help us.

Jesus knows how difficult it is to fight sin. He was a human being, so He knows how to help us. Jesus is our shelter. Any time we're afraid, or don't know what to do, we can run to Him.

Remember: We can run to Jesus any time we're afraid.

Jesus is our coach

December 20 Hebrews 12

Let us run the race that God has set before us. We need to keep our eyes on Jesus all the time. We should not give up. We can depend on Him from start to finish. (Heb. 12:1-2)

In any race, athletes must run their best. An athlete who looks around is not going to do his best. A good athlete looks straight ahead. He sees the finish line and runs as fast as he can to get there first.

As Christians, we're running a race for Jesus. We need to keep our eyes on Him all the time. He's waiting for us at the finish line. If we keep looking around, it won't be long before we slow down and start noticing the wrong things.

Jesus is our coach. He knows the track we're running on. He knows exactly what we have to do to win. All He asks is that we listen to His voice. We need to pray, read the Bible every day, and do what the Bible says. Then we will be good athletes. We run according to God's rules.

We should never take our eyes off Jesus. If we watch Him, we will be good athletes. We will finish the race and win first prize, because Jesus is waiting for us at the finish line.

Remember: Jesus is the best coach in the whole world.

We should only listen to Jesus

December 21 Hebrews 12

Now you have come to Zion, to the city of the living God. Thousands of joyful angels get together here every day. You have come to the place where the Lord's children will live forever. You have come to God Himself, who is the Judge of all people. You are with people who have been freed from their sins. You have come to Jesus. He gave us God's new covenant. His blood washes us clean from all sin. (Heb. 12:22-24)

All of us who believe in Jesus are on our way to a brand-new world. God, the most important Person of all, is there in heaven. All God's angels and all who have been washed clean by the blood of Jesus live there with Him. Jesus lives there, and He will make sure we're allowed into heaven.

Only people who believe in Jesus will be allowed into heaven. His blood makes us citizens of heaven. There is no other way to get to Jesus. Trying to live a good life doesn't impress the Lord. There is only one way to God. The Bible tells us that Jesus is the only way to God. We must listen to His voice every day. Then we will be safe and know that a brand-new life is waiting for us.

Remember: Only Jesus can make us children of God.

We will live with Jesus forever

December 22 Hebrews 13

Let us praise the Lord. Because we believe in Jesus, our lips must offer our sacrifice of praise to God. Let us glorify His Name. Don't forget to do good and to share what you have with those in need. Such sacrifices please God. (Heb. 13:15-16)

We need to glorify the Name of the Lord. We should be overflowing with joy. Our lips should be like a living sacrifice. Others should hear only good things from our mouths. They should hear that God is more important than anything else in our lives. They should also hear how great and good God is.

We shouldn't bring offerings to the Lord only with our lips. We should also bring offerings with our actions. The Lord wants us to do good deeds for Him. We shouldn't cling to our money. The Bible says that we should share what we have with others.

Do we share our money with others, or do we spend it all on ourselves? Of course, we can buy ourselves nice things. God doesn't get angry with us for doing that, but we can't be blind to the needs of people around us. We have to care for them. It's not only grown-ups who should help the needy. Children should do so, too.

Remember: We should serve the Lord with everything we have.

Jesus gives us everlasting life

December 23 1 John 5

I write this to you who believe in the Son of God, so that you may know you have eternal life. (1 John 5:13)

The apostle John wrote quite a few letters to believers. We can read three of these letters in the Bible. He explains why he has written the first letter—to tell readers that they have everlasting life.

The best words we can ever hear are the words from God's mouth that we belong to Him and that we are going to live forever. John says every human being on earth can hear these words. All we need to do is to put our hand into Jesus' hand and believe in Him. Then we can have everlasting life. It's as easy as that. We can't earn everlasting life or buy it with money. We have to believe in Jesus. Faith unlocks the road to life. We need to believe that Jesus died in our place, to pay for all our sins. Then we become God's children forever, and He is our Father forever.

Nobody who believes in Jesus will ever be disappointed. God tells us this. He takes care of everyone who belongs to Him. Because His children are very precious to Him, He leads us safely to heaven.

Remember: We need to believe that Jesus died for all our sins.

We need to ask Jesus to forgive us

December 24 1 John 1

If we say we have no sin, we are fooling ourselves. We are not telling the truth. But if we go to the Lord and ask Him to forgive us our sins, He will do it. God never lies. He keeps His promises. He takes away our sins. (1 John 1:8-9)

Sin is not obeying the Lord. If we know what the Lord wants us to do, and we don't listen, then we are sinning. Sin is going against the Lord's will.

Not even one Christian can say he or she never sins. People who say that are lying. What should we do with our sins? John says we should take them to the Lord. We need to tell Him that we're sorry for our sins. We have to ask the Lord to forgive us.

If we go to the Lord and say we're sorry, He forgives us our sins. This is a promise. He will never give our sins another thought.

We shouldn't allow our sins to stand between the Lord and us like a brick wall. We need to confess our sins and not do those things again. We should ask God to forgive us and then live a new life.

Remember: We need to ask the Lord to forgive our sins.

The Lord's children love one another

December 25 1 John 3

Dear children, let us stop just saying we love each other; let us really show it by our actions. (1 John 3:18)

John says that we can't say we love God if we hate His children. If we love God, we must love one another. God is love, and He loves all of us. That is why we should care for each other.

God shows His love in what He does for us. He let His Son die in our place. God doesn't just say He loves us. He shows it. If we look at Jesus, we can see exactly what love is.

As for us, we can't just say we love other Christians. We have to show it with everything we do and say. It doesn't do any good to pretend that we care for others. That's dishonest. We have really to care for each other and do kind things for each other. That's the way we show others what love is.

We shouldn't sit around and wait for people to be nice to us. We have to love them first and not stop, even if they don't thank us. We shouldn't expect thanks. As long as we do what God says, that's all that matters.

Remember: We need to show love to each other.

God is on His throne

December 26 Revelation 4

I was taken to heaven by the Spirit. I saw a throne in heaven. God was sitting on it! (Rev. 4:2)

The book of Revelation is written in picture language. When we read the words, we can form pictures in our minds of what we're reading. It tells us how God and Jesus hold the whole world in Their hands. In chapter 4, John takes us on a journey to heaven and shows us a picture of God sitting on His throne. God rules over everything and everybody. He is so powerful that nothing upsets Him.

His church and His creation surround God in heaven. John gives us a picture of the church as 24 elders, and of creation as four living beings. The Holy Spirit is also in heaven with God.

John sees the members of the Lord's church sitting in a circle around His throne. All of them are the same distance from God. No believer is closer or farther away from Him than any other.

God rules in heaven. Everybody in heaven worships God and bows before Him. Everyone is happy in heaven. God is King there.

Remember: We should thank the Lord that we are His children.

Jesus is the strongest in the whole world

December 27 Revelation 5

Then one of the believers in heaven said to me, "Stop crying. The Lion of the tribe of Judah has won. He alone can open the book in God's right hand." (Rev. 5:5)

While John was in heaven, he saw that God was holding a scroll in His hand, but the scroll was sealed. Nobody could open it. This upset John so much that he started crying. John knew that in the book God was holding in His right hand was the plan He had for the world. If nobody could open it, God's plan for the world would not work out.

One of the believers in heaven then told John to stop crying. There is Someone who can open the book in God's hand. He is the Lion, Jesus. When John looked up, he saw Jesus standing at the throne of God.

John says that Jesus stood there in heaven like a Lamb that had been slaughtered. The marks from His death on the cross were still on His body. John could see the scars the nails had made where they pierced His hands.

Jesus took the book from God's hand. He alone will bring about God's plan for the world. Jesus is now in control. The church in heaven was so happy about this that they fell down before Jesus. Everybody worshiped Him.

💡 **Remember:** Jesus is always in control.

Jesus punishes sinners

December 28 Revelation 6

As I watched, the Lamb broke the first of the seven seals on the scroll. (Rev. 6:1)

As John watched, Jesus broke the seals that kept the book shut, one by one. In picture language, John tells us that different horse riders are let loose next. They go into the world. The first horse is white. This is John's way of telling us that, right up to the very last day, there will be people who twist the Good News.

The color of the second horse is red. This represented war on earth. Until the day Jesus comes back to earth, people will fight wars against each other.

The third horse is black. John says this means that there will be a great famine on earth.

The color of the fourth horse is pale green, and its rider is called Death. From the time Jesus was taken up to heaven until His second coming, death will always be with us.

We shouldn't let these four horses and their riders frighten us. Jesus is there to take care of us.

Remember: God takes care of His children.

Everyone before God

December 29 Revelation 20

And anyone whose name was not found recorded in the Book of Life was thrown into the lake of fire. (Rev. 20:15)

John also tells us in Revelation what is going to happen on the very last day. He sees all the people on earth standing before the throne of God that day—old and young, big and small, the living and the dead. Nobody is left out. Then God opens all His books. All the deeds of people who didn't believe in Jesus are written down in these books—every single thing they did. All of these people are doomed. They will be thrown into the lake of fire. They'll stay there forever!

But there is another book, the Book of Life. In this book, God has written down the names of all His children. They will live forever in heaven.

God knows us either by our deeds or by our names. If He knows us because of what we do, we will spend the rest of our days being punished. But if God knows us by name, He will give us everlasting life.

When we believe in Jesus, He tears all our deeds out of His books.

Remember: We are going to live with Jesus one day.

We are going to live in God's new city

December 30 Revelation 21

I heard a loud shout from the throne, saying, "Look, the home of God is now among His people! He will live with them, and they will be His people. God Himself will be with them. He will remove all of their sorrows, and there will be no more death or sorrow or crying or pain. For the old world and its evils are gone forever." (Rev. 21:3-4)

God tells us in Revelation that He will come and live with us. His new address will be the same as ours.

Nothing bad will happen in God's new city. Nobody will die there. Nobody will cry. God Himself will wipe the tears from all eyes. There won't be any more pain and suffering. People will be safe in God's new city. There won't be any hospitals, because there won't be any more sick people.

In God's world, everything is brand-new. He keeps it all new Himself, forever. Here, on this earth, everything gets old. Things break. They don't last. Even the strongest people lose their strength, and the most active people become old and slow. But with God, none of this is going to happen. When we are with Him, we will always have something to celebrate. What a place to look forward to!

Remember: God will make a whole new world for us to live in.

Everybody is safe in God's new streets

December 31 Revelation 21-22

No temple could be seen in the city, for the Lord Almighty and the Lamb are its temple. (Rev. 21:22)

John gives us a quick peek at our last address. He shows us that God Himself is coming to live in the city. This new city has no temple, because God is there for everybody to see with their own eyes. The sun won't need to shine anymore, because the light coming from God is bright enough.

In God's new city, everyone is safe. No criminals or sinners are allowed there. There's enough food for everyone to eat. Nobody will ever go hungry.

In God's city, with its main street made of pure gold and its precious gems, all the people live together happily. No one fights, and there is no quarreling. Only God matters. Everyone bows before Him and praises Him.

When is God's new city going to be ready for us? We don't know. But Jesus tells us we need to invite Him. We need to ask Him to come back to us soon.

The early Christians often used the words "Marana tha." It was an invitation to the Lord. It means: "Come, O Lord!" "Marana tha"—"Come Lord Jesus!"

Remember: Invite Jesus to come back to us soon.